365 WAYS

to **Motivate** and **Reward** Your **Employees** Every Day With **Little** or **No Money**

Revised 2nd Edition

Dianna Podmoroff

365 WAYS TO MOTIVATE AND REWARD YOUR EMPLOYEES EVERY DAY — WITH LITTLE OR NO MONEY REVISED 2ND EDITION

Library of Congress Cataloging-in-Publication Data

Names: Podmoroff, Dianna, author.
Title: 365 ways to motivate and reward your employees every day with little or no money / Dianna Podmoroff.
Other titles: Three hundred and sixty-five ways to motivate and reward your employees every day with little or no money
Description: Revised 2nd edition. | Ocala, Florida : Atlantic Publishing Group, Inc., [2015] | Includes bibliographical references and index.
Identifiers: LCCN 2015037206| ISBN 9781620230695 (alk. paper) | ISBN 1620230690 (alk. paper)
Subjects: LCSH: Incentives in industry. | Employee motivation.
Classification: LCC HF5549.5.I5 P58 2015 | DDC 658.3/14--dc23 LC record available at http://lccn.loc.gov/2015037206

PROJECT MANAGER AND EDITOR: Rebekah Sack • rsack@atlantic-pub.com
INTERIOR LAYOUT AND JACKET DESIGN: Justin Oefelein • justin.o@spxmultimedia.com
COVER DESIGN: Jackie Miller • sullmill@charter.net

Reduce. Reuse.
RECYCLE.

A decade ago, Atlantic Publishing signed the Green Press Initiative. These guidelines promote environmentally friendly practices, such as using recycled stock and vegetable-based inks, avoiding waste, choosing energy-efficient resources, and promoting a no-pulping policy. We now use 100-percent recycled stock on all our books. The results: in one year, switching to post-consumer recycled stock saved 24 mature trees, 5,000 gallons of water, the equivalent of the total energy used for one home in a year, and the equivalent of the greenhouse gases from one car driven for a year.

Over the years, we have adopted a number of dogs from rescues and shelters. First there was Bear and after he passed, Ginger and Scout. Now, we have Kira, another rescue. They have brought immense joy and love not just into our lives, but into the lives of all who met them.

We want you to know a portion of the profits of this book will be donated in Bear, Ginger and Scout's memory to local animal shelters, parks, conservation organizations, and other individuals and nonprofit organizations in need of assistance.

– Douglas & Sherri Brown,
President & Vice-President of Atlantic Publishing

Table of Contents

Chapter 4: Understanding Employee Recognition 65

Chapter 5: Setting Up a Recognition Program 79

Introduction

Are you looking for new ideas to motivate your employees? This is the second edition of *365 Ways to Motivate and Reward Your Employees Every Day – With Little or No Money* with all updated motivational theories, techniques, and ideas to match the world we now live in.

In this newly revised edition, you will see more suggestions to use technology as gift ideas and motivational activities. The world today has gone digital as most people spend a lot of time on their cellphones, tablets, computers and, now, even watches — no matter if it's at work or at home. Take advantage of the technological suggestions throughout this edition, because they could get your employees moving!

A new motivational theory has also been added to this revised edition called the Four Drive Model Theory developed by Dr. Paul Lawrence and Dr. Nitin Nohria of the Harvard Business School. This theory goes beyond "money makes the world go 'round" idea and looks at different factors that motivate employees at their jobs. Emotions, actions, and materialistic measures are all discussed in this new theory in Chapter 2.

Example surveys that study employee motivation, satisfaction and engagement are also new features. If you're thinking about creating a similar survey for your employees, then take a look at how two major companies evaluated employees across the country. You might be surprised to find that money is not the most motivating factor for your employees.

This book still addresses the popular conversation topic that permeates most business productivity issues: employee motivation. Even the sharpest and most refined recruitment and hiring strategies are no match for the culprits of employee demotivation. At the root of the problem is the fact that you don't *find* motivated employees; you *provide motivating environments* for employees.

> "Motivated employees are found in lots of other workplaces, so why can't we find and hire them to work for us? We seem to have no end of qualified applicants, so we must be doing something right in recruitment and hiring. How come we can't seem to predict which employees will turn out to be star performers?"

Trying to motivate someone to do something is like putting the cart before the horse. You must first create an appealing and motivating work environment. After that, employees do what comes natural: they work hard for someone who recognizes and appreciates them. It would be pretty darn hard to come to work and do a slack job for a boss who supported you, encouraged you, respected you, and genuinely cared for you.

That exact notion is the foundation for this book. We still talk about ways to create a motivating culture that includes tips, techniques, and specific examples to for you to try. These techniques, though, are simply the tip of the motivation iceberg. They are the tangible rewards, activities, and recognitions that everyone sees. The real power of motivation lies in what is going on under the surface: how strong, how genuine, and how real is your commitment to provide meaningful and rewarding work? Ultimately, the question that remains is:

"How **motivated** are **YOU** to provide a **MOTIVATING WORKPLACE?**"

Chapter 1

Understanding Your Work Culture

Most employees start off with very good intentions, but it's common for their hard work to go unnoticed, and even unappreciated, day after day, month after month, and yes, sometimes even year after year — even the brightest star will begin to fade away.

It's not all dismal though; you have the power to motivate. Notice I said <u>motivate</u>, not coerce, force, cajole, badger or even convince. Motivation is not something that comes from the outside, and it can't be faked or put-on to please someone else. Zig Ziglar said it best when he stated that his role was not to motivate anyone: people motivate themselves. His job was to enlighten people and awake their enthusiasm.

It's common to want to do more for your employees' natural motivation and work habits. However, it's important to first understand the culture within your workplace before you try different techniques and exercises with your employees. This is so you don't waste time, become unproductive, or worse, make your employees even *more* unmotivated than before.

This book gives you 365 ideas to choose from so you don't make the mistake of forcing motivation in an unwanted form on your employees. We give you a plethora of ideas, activities, and techniques to choose from; one of them is bound to fit the culture within your workplace. And if you don't know what your workplace culture is, then we have solutions to help you figure that out, too.

My First Taste Of Motivational Culture

When I was first out of graduate school, fresh with my MBA in hand and convinced I knew everything I needed to know about managing people, I accepted a job at a manufacturing company. My job was to create and "be" the Human Resource department. During the interview process, it became clear that this company was struggling with a great many human resource issues that stemmed, in their opinion, from the fact that they had no professional human resource guidance.

Awesome, I thought… I was being handed a blank slate upon which I could work my magic. Clearly what this company needed were some HR systems and programs designed specifically for the company. I could do that.

In the first week, I learned a lot about manufacturing and about the history of the company and the issues management was struggling with. The first thing I learned was there were three distinct groups of people who worked there: managers, manager wanna-bes, and employees.

The managers talked incessantly about the problems created by the manager wanna-bes and the employees. They themselves, you see, were not employees — they were managers. As such, they had no responsibility for creating any problems; they just had to keep cleaning up the mess.

The manager wanna-bes were former "employees" who had been promoted to a supervisory position. This group complained incessantly about the employees and took every opportunity they could to make it clear to the employees that they wielded power and authority. What they pined for, however, was the prestige and status afforded to the managers.

Finally, we come to the employee group: the group without whose labor, the managers and manager wanna-bes would have no jobs. They complained incessantly to the managers about the manager wanna-bes. The main complaints were that the wanna-bes ruled with tyrannical power and were generally incompetent in the first place.

With my firm understanding of the long-entrenched pecking order within this company, I was called to a meeting with the director of operations, a well-intentioned man who could not figure out why his staff was so unmotivated. Sure, they met the production rates, but employee morale was in the toilet, absenteeism was rampant, supervisors were acting like vigilantes, and the management team was overwhelmed with the difficulties. As he explained all the programs he had put in place to improve motivation, I took notes:

- Free transportation to and from work (the facility was 45 minutes out of town)

- "Family tree" in the main entrance had pictures of all the employees hanging from its branches

- Compensation and benefits equivalent to other facilities within the company

- Suggestion box in the lunchroom

- Formal recognition program — employees earned points for company merchandise every month if production goals were met (they could win things like water bottles, T-shirts and sweatshirts, umbrellas, luggage, and the coveted leather bomber jacket)

- Annual company picnic

- Emphasis on equality and fairness

By the way, the "keeper" of equality and fairness was a manager who had been with the company since its inception. She had a photographic memory for details of who got what, what the circumstance was, what decision was made — every detail right down the color of socks the employee was wearing at the time I'm sure. This exacting recollection was useful, but more helpful was the fact that almost every incident that had ever occurred was etched in stone as a policy to be enacted in the exact same way should that circumstance ever reoccur.

I left the meeting ready to explore these motivation programs and perhaps improve them or develop new ones. The culture in this company was very strong, however, and as a manager, I was quickly indoctrinated into the manager's philosophy. I analyzed the motivation programs from this perspective and concluded that the programs were excellent; the problem was the supervisors.

We took immediate steps to improve the quality of supervision; the manager wanna-bes who could not get on board with treating their coworkers as humans were let go, and conditions seemed to improve for a while. But, in a relatively short period of time, absenteeism slowly started to creep up, and morale went down again. So much for my theory about the supervisors!

We tried new programs like birthday recognitions, pizza once a month, monthly newsletters, an absenteeism program where employees could earn even more company merchandise, safety recognition awards, employee of the month — you name it, we tried it.

The problem, which seems so obvious to me now, was that the attitudes and general work environment did not change. The managers were still the managers, the wanna-bes were still the wanna-bes, and the employees were still at the bottom of the food chain. There was motivation all right; unfortunately, it was aimed at keeping everyone else in check. The humanity was gone, and it wasn't until I looked at the motivation programs from an employee's perspective that I realized the magnitude of the problem.

☹ Free transportation—Great. You don't pay us enough to afford and insure a car, so how else are we supposed to get to work?

☹ "Family tree"—How lame. This is the most dysfunctional family we've ever seen, and you have pictures up there of employees who quit months, even years, ago.

☺ Compensation and benefits—Yeah — when you explained how "great" our total compensation was, you included almost $2.00 per hour for the "free" transportation we get!

☹ Suggestion box in the lunchroom—The box that has no paper or pens and that gets read once in a blue moon and if a suggestion is implemented one of the wanna-bes will likely get the credit? Great.

☹ Formal recognition program—The production goals aren't goals. They are what we need to produce — period. The manager gets the sales forecast, determines what we need to produce, and we do it. And our work gets other people rewarded — we make the production goal, and everyone in the company gets points. Why bother? Just give us the stuff so we'll wear your name all over town, and then everyone's happy.

☺ Annual Company picnic—OK, this one's quite fun, but we get it every year regardless of how well we do — the managers certainly wouldn't miss the opportunity.

☹ Emphasis on equality and fairness—Yeah, I just love it when I ask for a special consideration and it's denied only because someone three years ago asked for the same thing and it didn't work out. Or, I come to work on time every day and I get treated exactly the same as the guy who misses a quarter of his shifts... wouldn't want to be unfair... wouldn't want to upset the slackers... they deserve the same as the rest of us... wouldn't want to use common sense to deal with anything... it's much better to have a thousand policies in place — just in case.

I know, I know… I'm mortified when I look back on this and think how completely snowed I was. I saw only what was on the surface (the tip of the motivation iceberg) and had no appreciation for the enormity of what was lurking below. The attitudes, beliefs, and values of company management formed the foundation of this enormous issue and since only the reactions (the attempts to motivate) were visible, those were identified as the problem.

Also, remember that I came into the company as a complete newbie. I had no preconceived notions or ideas about the way things had always been, but I was so quickly absorbed into the strong counter-motivating culture that I didn't even realize it was happening. This brings the challenge of motivation into perspective. Imagine how difficult it is for people who work in, and perhaps built, the company environment to identify the underlying issues that de-motivate, let alone come up with solutions that address what is both above and below the surface. Motivation is not an issue that can be fixed with a "solution." Workplace motivation is bred and nurtured, and it involves all parties and all aspects of the work environment.

Motivation encompasses the entire scope of workplace activities from the actual work being performed to who is performing the work and how the work is managed — all of these aspects significantly contribute to the health of the workplace and thus to the level of what is commonly termed "employee motivation." This is a complex topic that affects the performance of the company as a whole, and it impacts the level of satisfaction of each and every employee.

After reading this book, you will have a new-found appreciation for the importance and complexity of workplace motivation, and you will be armed with the tools you need to start building a high motivation workplace within your organization.

"Workplace motivation is bred and nurtured, and it involves all parties & all aspects of the work environment."

The benefits of a highly motivated workforce are very evident. The transformation will not happen overnight, but when it does, you can expect the following results:

- Renewed motivation, morale, and meaning
- Improved personal/professional performance
- Enhanced teamwork, trust, and fun
- Increased energy and resilience to stress
- Enriched quality of work/life balance
- Heightened workplace creativity and humor
- Enlightened and inspired organizations
- Enhanced retention through recognition
- Elevated enthusiasm and involvement with interactive sessions
- Deepened appreciation for internal and external customers
- Improved customer care and service delivery
- Decreased absenteeism, burnout, and turnover
- Improved productivity and organization

The benefits of well-directed motivation are obvious and compelling and thus my intention with this book is twofold:

1. To heighten your awareness of and appreciation for the issues lurking beneath the surface of your workplace and give you tools to **build a strong motivation foundation**

2. To inspire you with specific tools, techniques, and strategies for building a **high motivation workplace full of motivated employees**

In the next chapter, we will take an in-depth look at motivation — what it is and what it is not.

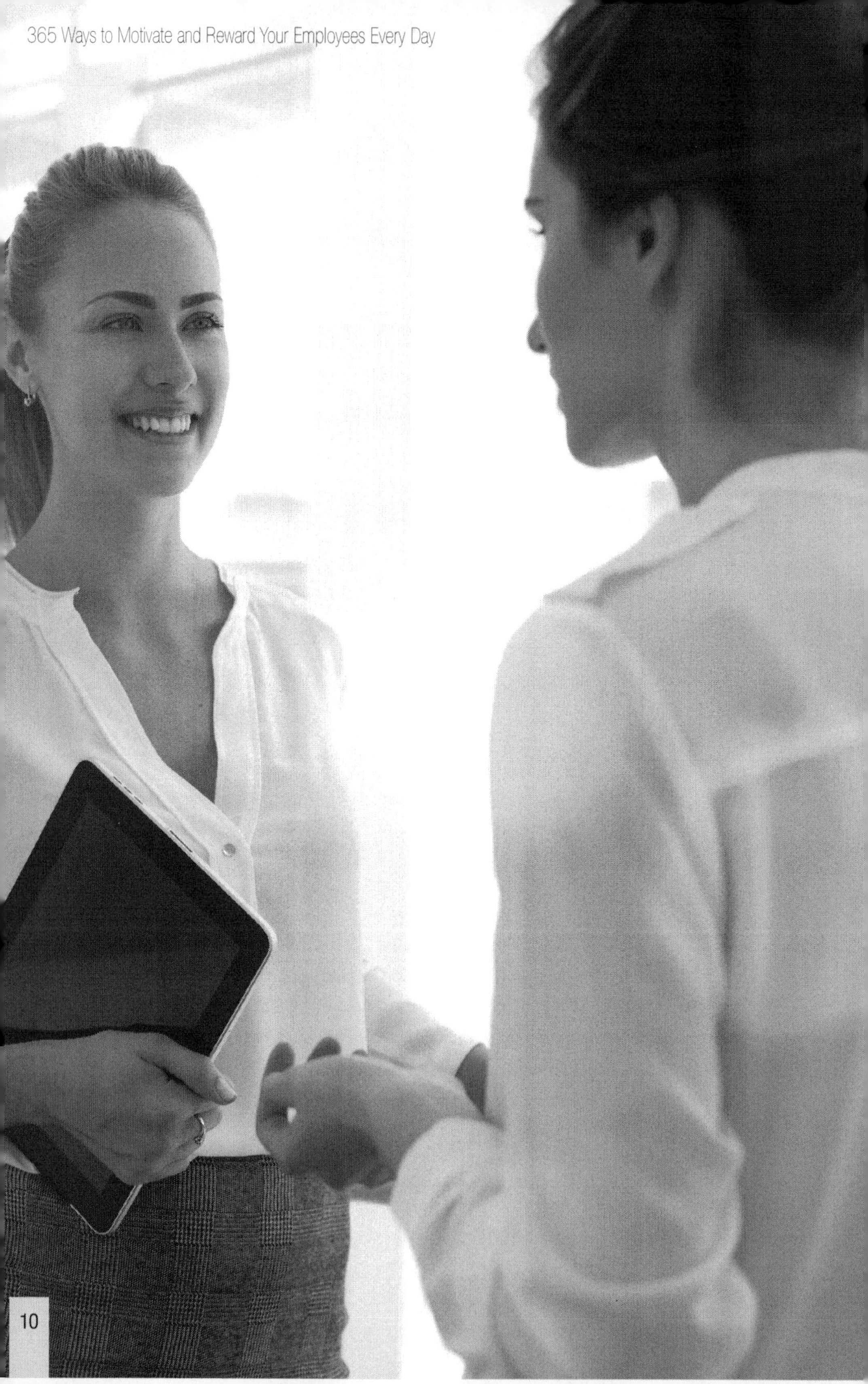

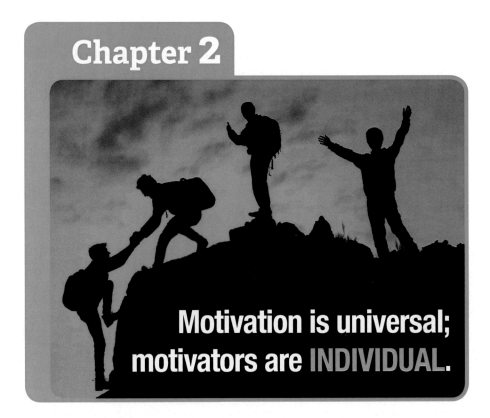

Chapter 2

Motivation is universal;
motivators are INDIVIDUAL.

The History of Motivation

Human beings are pre-wired to be motivated. Something gets us up every morning. Even if the only reason we get up is because we're hungry, we're still motivated to satisfy our need to eat. In the workplace, motivation is more complex and what motivates some does not motivate others. Therein lies the problem that managers struggle with on a daily basis. Often deemed as "attitude" problems, these issues are usually problems related to untapped or misdirected motivation. In order to correct the problem, it is important that managers and leaders understand exactly what motivation is. Once you understand the forces at work, you will have a much easier time applying the techniques and tips presented in the subsequent chapters.

There are many different theories of motivation that have become intertwined with current management practices. In order to get a solid grasp on this concept of motivation in general, it is important that we revisit, and in some cases learn about, some of these foundational theories. These will help us to understand why we have come to view workplace motivation as we have and where some of the common solutions to motivational problems come from.

Motivation Theory #1: Abraham Maslow

The desire to satisfy a need is what Dr. Abraham Maslow identified as the impetus for our attitudes and actions. According to Maslow, we have five levels of need.

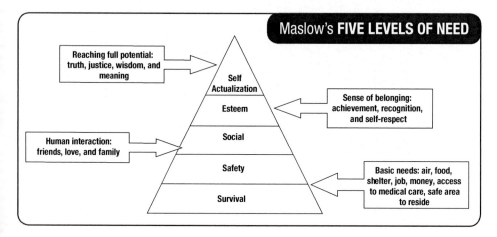

Since we spend nearly one-third of our adult lives at work, it stands to reason that we want our workplace to be a source of need fulfillment. When that happens, our lives are full and enriched, and we can focus our attention on finding meaning through work; when it doesn't happen, we are too preoccupied with finding other ways to satisfy our needs that we are never truly "present" at work. Our productivity, engagement, morale, enthusiasm, interest, and enjoyment all suffer. Put a whole bunch of unfulfilled people in one workplace and look out…

Many recognition programs are based on Maslow's theory. Attempts to satisfy needs related to social interaction and self-esteem are commonly put in place. One of the most common motivation tools used today is the "employee of the month" or some variation thereof. These types of tools are a direct response to our belief that employees seek workplace recognition of their accomplishments, and this recognition helps satisfy self-esteem needs. The theory follows that if we are not recognized for our achievements, then we are not growing and fully developing as individuals, and our attentions may wander away from the tasks at hand.

Maslow's work is often considered the foundation from which other motivation theories grew.

Motivation Theory #2: Frederick Herzberg

As mentioned, Maslow is considered the "father" of motivational theory and most of the subsequent work on motivation has been done with his model in mind. Frederick Herzberg's Hygiene and Motivational Factors theory was the next to emerge. He took Maslow's ideas and concentrated on human needs at work, not for life in general. His theory centered on the notion that humans have two types of needs: (1) needs related to hygiene and (2) needs related to motivational factors.

Hygiene factors are those elements of a job that are related to working conditions, and motivational factors relate to elements that enrich one's job.

Herzberg's Hygiene and Motivational Factors	
Hygiene Factors	**Motivational Factors**
Policies and practices	Recognition
Compensation	Achievement
Job security	Advancement
Coworkers	Growth
Supervision	Responsibility

Hygiene factors themselves are not motivating, but if they are not adequate, they are sources of dissatisfaction. All hygiene factors must be met in order for motivational factors to be satisfying. Herzberg coined the term "job satisfaction" and referred to it as the designing of jobs with built-in motivational factors.

The response to Herzberg's two-factor theory within corporations was to concentrate on the actual design of jobs being performed. A great deal of attention was given to making sure people had jobs that were inherently satisfying. The burden of workplace motivation was solidly entrenched as the responsibility of management, and they were tasked with making sure employee needs were taken care of.

These theories made sense and were empirically supported, but unfortunately, workplace motivation did not necessarily improve as a result of any changes these theories supported. Some people were motivated, some weren't, and it seemed the increased understanding of motivation was doing little to help the practical application of motivation at work.

So, a whole new generation of motivational theorists emerged. These theorists found that Maslow's hierarchy did not work in the real world. The needs that Maslow identified seemed well grounded, but most people skipped around through the levels depending on their circumstances, stage of life, interests, etc. They cited many examples that were not congruent with the hierarchy. If you consider a starving artist who sacrifices certain survival and safety needs in order to pursue his passion, or a physician who gives up her practice to work with children in Africa whose mothers have AIDS, then you can understand that a hierarchical set-up is not consistent with human behavior.

The difficulty with Herzberg's two-factor theory was with the overlap of hygiene and motivation factors. They were not quite as black and white as the theory suggested, and dissatisfaction with one factor could have very different effects with different people. Some people did not respond to increased recognition (motivation factor) but instead focused on advancement. Others were willing to sacrifice compensation (hygiene factor) for work that provided a great deal of personal satisfaction.

Again, the theories fell short of applying to the workforce in general.

Motivation Theory #3: Clayton Alderfer

To address the shortcomings in Maslow's model, Clayton Alderfer developed the Existence/Relatedness/Growth (ERG) Theory of Needs. He took Maslow's ideas and created three groups of needs that individuals could move through simultaneously. He also proposed that different people would move thorough the needs in different orders.

Existence/Relatedness/Growth (ERG)	
Need	**Example**
Existence	This group of needs is concerned with providing the basic requirements for material existence. It includes Maslow's Survival and Safety needs. Working to earn money to buy food, clothing, and shelter satisfies existence needs.
Relationship	This group of needs centers on the desire to establish and maintain interpersonal relationships. These needs are related to Maslow's Social needs. Since we spend a significant time at work we look to coworkers and colleagues to satisfy many of our social needs.
Growth	These needs are satisfied through personal growth and development opportunities. They are related to the group of needs Maslow referred to as Esteem and Self-Actualization. Many of us look to marry our personal meaning and purpose with our professional lives and thus our job becomes a main source of satisfaction or dissatisfaction.

According to Alderfer, people can move simultaneously through the needs, but lower level (existence) needs will take on greater importance when higher level need achievement is frustrated. This dynamic is called "frustration-regression" and works like this: If a higher level need is left unfulfilled or appears unattainable, the individual will seek out lower level needs, because they are easier to satisfy. This regression exacerbates the frustration because less time is spent trying to pursue those needs that result in the most personal satisfaction.

Practical solutions based on this theory concentrated on making sure the lower level needs were satisfied for everyone before moving on to higher needs. The intention was to create workplaces that did not frustrate or hinder employees' search for satisfaction.

Motivation Theory #4: Victor Vroom

Vroom's theory is based on the idea that individuals have expectations about outcomes and that, in terms of work, there are two main groups of outcomes:

1. **Intrinsic outcomes/motivators:** This is how interesting, challenging, and meaningful the job is.

2. **Extrinsic outcomes/rewards:** Work related conditions, salary, and security are the expected outcomes or rewards.

Vroom's theory assumes that behavior results from conscious choices and that people are naturally wired to maximize pleasure (positive outcomes) and minimize pain (negative outcomes). The expectancy theory says that individuals have different goals/desires/dreams and they can be motivated if they believe all of the following to be true:

1. There is a correlation between their effort and performance — the harder they work, the greater their performance.

2. Greater performance will result in a desired outcome (reward).

3. That outcome (reward) will satisfy a need (desire/ dream/goal).

4. The desire to satisfy that need is strong enough to justify the increased effort.

For expectancy theory to work, all four of those beliefs must be present for an employee to motivate him or herself to put forth the necessary effort.

The easiest way to understand Expectancy Theory is with an example as follows:

Bobby goes to work every day and earns a decent living. Raises at his company are given out on a yearly basis based solely on tenure (length of time with the company). Bobby does not have to put forth any excess effort to earn his raise; he simply has to show up for work every day for another year. **For this company, pay increases are not motivating, and they have no ability to motivate.**

Susan also goes to work every day and earns a decent living. At Susan's company, wage increases are based on performance. Each employee sets objectives for the year, and they are evaluated on how well they achieved their goals. Because the employees are involved in the goal-setting process, they are excited about and committed to completing them. They also know that pay raises are linked directly to performance. This ups the ante so to speak, and the employees are doubly motivated: 1) they are intrinsically motivated to achieve goals they have set for themselves, and 2) there is potential for a monetary reward if they achieve their goal. **Money is a motivator in this company, but it is important to note it is not the sole motivator.**

As you can see, the performance-based models of compensation are a direct result of Vroom's theory, as are all the other incentive programs that are so popular today.

Motivation Theory #5: Graves and Beck

A theory that has direct implications for workplace motivation is Spiral Dynamics. Spiral Dynamics explores the core values and thoughts that drive individual's beliefs and actions. The original concept began back in the 1930s with the work of Dr. Clare Graves, but he died before publishing his theory, and it remained in the realm of personality psychologists until Dr. Don Beck wrote a book entitled "Spiral Dynamics Integral" based on his extended version of the Graves' original biopsychosocial theory.

In Beck's model, Graves' value systems are combined with memes (cognitive or behavioral pattern that can be transmitted from one individual to another one) to form nine different ^{V}MEMEs (or vMemes) and by discovering which ^{V}MEME an individual operates under, others can relate better to that individual.

Note: According to **www.spiraldynamics.org**, "The term ^{V}MEME (or vMeme) is an effort to show the connection between (a) the ideas carried in memes and (b) the underlying thinking systems, value systems, worldviews, coping systems, Spiral colors, or Gravesian levels of psychological existence. Some people who should know better still insist on confusing the two domains. [...] Memes and ^{V}Memes are not the same thing."

The memes are presented in a helix model that indicates the movement through the levels but also recognizes that people may move back down or stay fixed depending on life circumstances. In Spiral Dynamics, the goal is for all people to continue their movement upward in the spiral, continually expanding their thoughts and consciousness, but that existential side of Spiral Dynamics will not be explored in this book.

Eight Value Systems / ᵛMEMEs that have emerged to date:

ᵛMEMEs	Description
BEIGE	**Instinctive/Survivalist** Do what you must to survive.
PURPLE	**Magical/Animistic** Use rituals and have a mystical sense of cause and effect.
RED	**Impulsive/Egocentric** Emphasize cunning and doing what you want to do. Strong prevail and the weak serve.
BLUE	**Purposeful/Authoritarian** Desire ordered existence and enforce principles based on what is "right." Controlled by a higher power.
ORANGE	**Strategic/Achievement Oriented** Take advantage of all opportunities and strive for success. Make things better and bring prosperity.
GREEN	**Egalitarian/Community Oriented** Demand human rights and develop caring communities. Look for affiliation and sharing.
YELLOW	**Integrative** View the world as integrated systems and emphasize flexibility. Change is the norm.
TURQUOISE	**Holistic** Combine mind and spirit to experience life's complete existence. The world is a delicate balance that is in jeopardy in human hands.
CORAL	**Undefined** *We're not there yet.*

Essentially, Spiral Dynamics was developed in order to help us understand the following:

- How people think *about* things (as opposed to "what" they think)
- Why people make decisions in different ways
- Why people respond to different motivators
- Why and how values arise and spread
- The nature of change

Spiral Dynamics is the theory that attempts to address why some motivation programs work for some people in specific situations. The other main theories attempt to uncover the one universal method for motivating people whereas Spiral Dynamics takes a much more individualized approach to motivation. Because it has been my experience that people respond to motivational methods very differently, the premises of this theory are evident in many of the constructs of workplace motivation presented in this book.

Motivation Theory #6: Lawrence and Nohria

The Four Drive Theory of Human Nature, created in 2002 by two Harvard Business School professors, is the most recent motivation model. It's a holistic way of looking at employee motivation beyond the typical "pay" model that most corporate businesses use today.

Lawrence and Nohria researched four drives that motivate employees, and each one plays an important part in how organizational leaders understand their staff. They are:

1. **Acquire & Achieve:** Employees are driven to acquire things, status, and resources. This is the drive that most companies focus on by using cash incentives and base pay.

2. **Bond & Belong:** Employees are driven to create positive bonds, engage and fit in. For example,

some companies do not actively encourage employees to participate in team building activities. This model shows that Bond & Belong relates directly to team building, because it influences employees' motivation.

3. **Create & Challenge:** Employees are driven to attain mastery, to learn, to improve, and to create. This drive highlights the fact that employees are engaged on the job and are not bored or doing nothing. Instead of always looking for ways to make work easier, leaders should look for ways to challenge their employees. This gives them the opportunity to learn and grow at their job, and it encourages leaders to look at the structure of their jobs, projects, and incentives.

4. **Defend & Define:** Employees are driven to defend status, ideas, and relationships and to define purpose. This regards a company's reputation, moral bearing, and culture (among other things) that are all important factors in employee motivation. Most company leaders do not think Defend & Define plays part in employee motivation, but it does. It can be portrayed by an entire company or by smaller departments.

All four of the drives are important to employee motivation, but if not implemented properly, they can be destructive. They can cause too much competition between co-workers, which will then lead to other issues.

The balance among all four drives is what makes this theory successful; if not, it may do more harm than good.

How Motivation Theories Apply to You

All of these theories of motivation are useful for constructing an overall answer to a fundamental workplace issue: how to put the right people in the right positions and help them reach maximum satisfaction and achieve maximum productivity.

That really is what motivation is all about. You can try, try, and try some more to motivate someone to do something, but if he or she has no desire (gets no satisfaction) to do the task, then you are beating a dead horse.

Effective motivation requires shifting your mindset and understanding that you can't make anyone do anything. What you can do is create the right set of circumstances for a motivating workplace to emerge. That is what this book will teach you to do.

You **can't coerce motivation** but you can, and should, **foster it.**

As you have seen with the varying motivation theories, many people have tried to define motivation. However, for our purposes, we are focusing on motivation in the workplace; therefore, **motivation is the inner force that drives individuals to achieve personal and professional goals**.

Why is workplace motivation so important? We need motivated employees in order to survive. Motivated employees are more productive, and they infuse positive energy into the work environment. There is nothing more de-motivating than an unhappy workplace, and negativity is an insidious and nefarious opponent in the struggle for a high-motivation work environment. Add to that the fact that what motivates employees changes constantly, and it is no wonder workplace motivation is one of the most complex issues managers deal with on a daily basis.

Because workplace motivation is on the minds of organizational leaders everywhere, there is considerable misinformation about motivation that needs to be cleared up. To get the ball rolling, here are some common motivation myths.

Common Motivation Myths

"I am an upbeat, motivational kind of guy, and I can motivate others."

As much as we would like it to be true, no one can really motivate anyone else: they have to motivate themselves. What you can do is create a motivating environment for each of your employees.

"Money is the universal motivator."

While this is a common belief, it is not true. Unfair or inadequate compensation is a significant factor in employee dissatisfaction, but good or extra compensation does not encourage people to be more motivated than they already are. Employee motivations are highly sophisticated and complex, and your job is to figure out what motivates whom and then deliver it.

"The best motivator I know is fear — fear of losing a job should motivate anyone."

Fear may motivate in the very short-term, but it does nothing to enhance workplace harmony, and it goes a long way toward creating employee dissatisfaction. No one wants to work for a boss who is threatening and intimidating (at least not for long), and you'll find yourself with a steady stream of new and untrained employees if this is your tactic of choice.

"I know what motivates me, so I know what motivates my employees."

Wrong! Everyone is motivated by different things at different times. What works for you may or may not work for your employees, and what works for them today may or may not motivate them tomorrow. Motivation isn't simple, but it is so worth the trouble of finding out what individual employee's triggers are.

"Increased job satisfaction means increased job performance."

While I've alluded to this relationship throughout the book so far, the relationship between job satisfaction and job performance is not 100 percent correlated. Just because an employee is motivated to do a good job and perform to his potential does not mean that he will perform to the expectations of the organization. There are many other factors that a company's management must attend to, such as aligning workplace goals with personal goals, ensuring employees have access to the tools and resources required to do a great job, and communicating expectations clearly, concisely, and consistently. Providing a motivation-rich environment serves as the foundation for a high performance workplace.

I'm sure you yourself have espoused one or more of these ideas, and they are very much a part of mainstream managerial thought. The problem is they are also some of the main reasons why workplace motivation continues to frustrate managers from every industry and every type of organization. By virtue of being aware of these common pitfalls, you can start to combat them within your organization right now. However, knowing what motivation *is not* is only the first step. Now, you need to develop a solid understanding of what motivation *is* and why companies and researchers across the world are so interested in the subject.

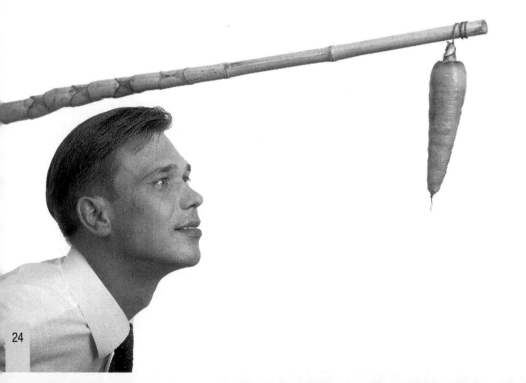

Chapter 3

Employee Motivation

Building a Strong, Motivation-Based Foundation

We have already defined motivation as the *inner force that drives individuals to achieve personal and professional goals,* but employee motivation must also be viewed from two different perspectives: internal and external motivators.

Internal Motivators

The internal motivators are what influence and propel an individual to pursue a certain job, type of career, education, or other activity. These inner drives provide people with their most basic form of satisfaction. A person who feels an overwhelming desire to be a musician will never be completely fulfilled in an office job regardless of the motivation tips and tricks used. Or, the person who desires order and structure will never find complete fulfillment in a job that is unstructured. In order to provide a high-motivation workplace, you must be aware of, and sensitive to, these baseline motivators that affect your employees on a day-to-day basis.

> ### INTERNAL MOTIVATORS:
> aspects of work that generally compel a person to decide to seek a particular type of employment in a particular industry.

These internal motivators are resistant to change or outside influence. This is why it is so crucial to build an environment and culture that understands and respects the different motivational forces of its employees at different times. When an employee is working at a job he or she is highly interested in or passionate about, your job as manager/ motivator/coach is that much smoother. Rather than embarking on an uphill battle trying to mold an employee into one who loves his position, you need to create a workplace that is dedicated to finding out what its employees need and then commit to providing it.

The simplest way to approach the task is to hire for motivational fit in the first place. If you hire people who possess internal motivational factors that are easily satisfied through the type of work offered, the goals of your organization, or the type of management you provide, then achieving a high motivation workplace is not too difficult.

Hiring the right person for the right job is always the goal, but we know that the selection is far from perfect, so when we have employees who are struggling to find their motivation, we need to create flexibility in our workplace and accommodate those individuals the best we can. We can't change anyone's current internal motivators, but we can provide options that help the person to find an internally motivating role within the company.

External Motivators

The external motivators consist of those things that the world offers in response to an individual's inner drives. These can be considered the enticements an employer offers to its employees such as salary, benefits, recognition, and advancement. These external motivators are what we commonly think of when we talk about factors of job satisfaction that improve employee motivation.

EXTERNAL MOTIVATORS:
aspects of work that generally compel a person to seek or maintain employment with a particular company.

Here are some basic external motivators:

- Opportunity to work and apply special gifts and abilities in an employment setting

- Wages that enable employees to provide themselves basic necessities and some luxuries such as the purchase of a home or travel

- Means to save for and enjoy old age

- Provision of medical and other insurance coverage

- Camaraderie with coworkers

- Recognition of work done

- Acknowledgment and possible reward for special contributions

- Opportunity for advancement

- Opportunity for self-development

- Opportunity for continuous learning (improve skills, knowledge, education)

- Realization of one's full potential

Remember, however, that these external motivators are not direct substitutes for an employee's inner drives, but when employees are working in positions that are not the best fit for them, in terms of their internal motivators, these external aspects of a job can and need to be used as mitigating factors.

What Employees Find Motivating

In 2014, Employee engagement firm TinyPulse conducted an employee survey titled, "The 7 Key Trends Impacting Today's Workplace." The firm researched a variety of management topics, including what motivates employees, and involved 200,000 employees from more than 500 organizations.

The results of the motivation questionnaire shocked TinyPulse leaders and entrepreneurs across the country, because money was not the most motivating factor.

These are the responses:

Camaraderie, peer motivation	20%
Intrinsic desire to do a good job	17%
Feeling encouraged and recognized	13%
Having a real impact	10%
Growing professionally	8%
Meeting client/customer needs	8%
Money and benefits	7%
Positive supervisor/senior management	4%
Believe in the company/product	4%
Other	9%

When asked to elaborate on their No. 1 motivator, employee responses included a lot of praise about the support they give each other. According to a few responses published on the survey, employees' peers motivate them to excel, go the extra mile for one another, and actively support and participate in team projects.

Given the major role co-workers play in motivating one another, it's up to hiring mangers to keep the positive environment between their employees when they hire new ones, TinyPulse concluded. And it's true — in order to keep the cultural fit within your workplace, you need to not only look at people's skills and academic achievements, but their personality, too. If one person isn't contributing to the positive energy within a department, group, or team, then the motivational energy could disappear.

As a team leader, don't forget to harness the positive energy your employees portray into every activity — or other departments if you're in charge of multiple — to see great outcomes within your company.

> "Continuous, supportive communications from managers, supervisors and associates is too often underemphasized. It's a major, major motivator."
>
> **-Jim Moultrup**
> **Management consultant**

Work is all about the people. You can develop the most fancy and sophisticated programs for enticing people to work in the company's best interest, but if you don't place value on the best interests of your people, then all is for naught.

The Motivation Dilemma

When we talk about motivation, we need to remember that we are talking about motivating individual people who each bring a unique set of skills and other personal factors with them to work every day. To build a strong foundation for a motivating culture, you need to understand the power and complexity of the internal factors that motivate each of these peoples' behavior.

Using our iceberg analogy, the internal motivators are the core factors that lay beneath the surface of any workplace environment. These core factors can either support motivation and boost morale, job-satisfaction, productivity, and profitability; or they can sink the entire organization. An iceberg that doesn't have a strong foundation will eventually melt away, but those that have deep roots can remain floating for centuries. For organizations, what determines the difference is the level of commitment to providing a motivating work environment that supports rather than quells its employees' natural motivation to do a good job. Yes, that's right — employees are naturally motivated to do a good job. People don't take on tasks or responsibilities with the intention of doing them poorly. When they do a poor job, it is not because they lack motivation; it's because they have misdirected or misguided motivation.

But, if people are *naturally* motivated to do a good job, why do managers from all industries, all sizes of business, and all organizational structures continue to ask: How do you motivate people? How can we motivate our people toward improved productivity? How can we motivate for more effective performance?

They ask these questions because they have yet to accept that people are already motivated. They might not be motivated to move in the "right" direction or they might not have the "right" motivators; but they are motivated.

People are always motivated, and they will remain **so as long as they are alive.**

By asking the question, "How do you motivate employees?" you are approaching the problem from the wrong perspective. The question begs to be answered with a one-size-fits-all solution. Everyone is looking for that one perfect methodology that is guaranteed to work. Managers want to know the secret formula for motivation because their belief is that their employees will magically do what they want, in the way they want it, and enjoy doing it, too. Unfortunately, given all the research and brain-power of the talented individuals who have worked toward this end, if a motivational panacea existed, it would have been found by now.

Job enrichment, incentive programs, management by objective, self-directed work teams, performance-based pay, participative management — I could go on and on — but these systems have all been proposed and hailed as the ultimate method to achieve motivation-rich environments with soaring productivity. Have any of them proven that they are the answer? No. And we can keep looking for that one miracle cure for what we call "lack of motivation."

Each of these systems, and any others that we come up with in the future, work extremely well for some, modestly for others, and not at all for the rest. People who are intensely competitive may respond well to performance-based pay. But for those who are more interested in working as a team and collaborating on projects, performance-based pay is a dismal failure. The application of performance-based pay is not the problem; the problem is that it is not motivating to all people at one time nor is it motivating to some people all of the time. What inevitably happens is that the organization's leaders decide that performance-based pay does not work, and they go on a never-ending search for a method that will. They jump from one system to the next not realizing that the changing systems are causing as much, if not more, problems for their employees and managers.

When we talk about motivation, it's not just employees we have to consider — the managers and leaders are also influenced by the changes. Their motivational levels change from time to time and from circumstance to circumstance. Managers, just like their subordinates who were content with the old system, may respond negatively or not at all to the changes, and they will vary in their ability to apply the new system effectively. Add to that the fact that employees who were considered motivated and productive under the old system may become unmotivated and unhappy with the changes, and you have the exact reason why trying to find a motivational cure-all will never work. The act of looking for an answer to the question, "How do you motivate employees?" puts you in a vicious cycle where some people are happy some of the time, but no one is happy all of the time.

When tackling the issue of employee motivation you need to reframe your question:

How should Manager X manage Employee Y to do Z?

Four Interrelated Work Systems

When you restructure your approach to employee motivation and ask, "How should Manager X manage Employee Y to do Z?" you acknowledge the four main contributors to workplace motivation and performance:

1. Management Methods

The managerial policies and practices accepted and endorsed by the organization, its values, and culture.

2. The Management

The beliefs, values, personality, capabilities, etc. that influence the actions of each manager, leader, and supervisor within the organization.

3. The Managed

The beliefs, values, personality, capabilities, etc. that influence the way each employee within the organization desires to be managed and his reactions to the current management style.

4. The Work

The actual work that needs to be done within the organization to ensure sustainability and/or profitability.

"There must be congruency between the character of the work to be done, the psychology of the person who is managing, the psychology of the people being managed and the methods and procedures of management."

-From the Historical Collection of the work of Dr. Clare W. Graves, William R. Lee, August 2003

For a motivation-rich culture to emerge, all four of these factors must be aligned for each and every employee within the company. That is no small task, and that is why motivation continues to be one of the hottest managerial topics to date.

If you think of these systems as cogs in the wheel of the entire management system, you begin to see that if any one of them falls out of sync, the system as a whole suffers.

In order to fully appreciate the impact of each of the systems, let's examine each one and the implications for workplace motivation separately.

Management methods

Management methods are those practices within the organization's toolkit that managers use to oversee, supervise, direct, reward, and correct subordinate's work and behavior. Different companies implement multiple management methods that they believe will address workplace motivation. Most of them adopt a mix of two or three methods that best suits the organization's values, beliefs, and goals. However, remember assuming that one or more of these methods will motivate employees is a common mistake. Different rewards motivate people differently, and the trick is figuring out which ones motivate the employees in your specific organization.

You must not forget that the method of management is but one of the four interrelated dynamics operating within any workplace at any time. Therefore, if you attack motivational issues by addressing only one aspect of the workplace dynamic, you will not see the broad scope results you are hoping for. What you do need to have is a good understanding of how these various management methods work and what aspects of employee motivation they most appeal to. When you understand why these programs have been proposed, you can then decide which ones to apply in which situations and with which employees.

Here is a summary of some of the most popular management methods intended to increase employee motivation and performance:

Management by objective

Management by objective (MBO) is a management method developed by Peter Drucker that advocates a participative goal-setting process that actively involves managers and subordinates at every level in the organization. Objectives are agreed to and decided upon between management and employees so employees know what is expected of them. Employees work on objectives that are directly tied to organizational goals, which helps them set individual goals as well. Then, these individual objectives form the basis of the performance review process for both the manager and the employee.

The key elements of MBO are:

- Effective planning and goal setting by top management.

- Setting of individual goals that are directly related to the organization's goals.

- Employees are given autonomy in developing and selecting means for achieving objectives.

- Employee performance in relation to objectives is regularly reviewed.

The principal behind MBO is that it encourages employees to appraise their own performance through a process of shared set goals and evaluation. Employees understand the goals of the organization, and they see how their performance affects the company as a whole, thus creating a group of individuals who all have one higher purpose in mind. MBO creates a link between top management's strategic thinking and the strategy's implementation lower down. Responsibility for objectives is passed from the organization to its individual members.

Closely related to MBO is the development of SMART goals:

Specific: the target is clearly defined.

Measurable: the target state has a quantitative component that can be verified numerically.

Appropriate: the employee has the means and resources available to accomplish the goal or meet the objective.

Realistic: the employee, after considering likely extenuating circumstances, has a reasonable chance of success.

Time-bound: the target state has a specified time for completion.

The principle behind management by objective is to increase the motivational factors such as autonomy, responsibility, and direct involvement in setting work goals. Upper management typically drives traditional workplaces, and their strategies and objectives are handed out from the top down. Basically, the higher the position one has within the corporate hierarchy, the more responsibility and autonomy they have. MBO seeks to do the opposite and drive the decision-making downward, allowing employees at all levels of the organization to contribute meaningfully to goal setting.

Job enrichment and rotation

Job enrichment is a type of job redesign that is intended to address the effects of boredom, lack of flexibility, and employee dissatisfaction that result from work tasks that are repetitive and highly directed. We know that responsibility and autonomy are important job-satisfaction factors, so with job enrichment, the scope of a job is vertically expanded to provide a greater variety of tasks that require self-sufficiency.

This management method stems from Herzberg's work in the 1950s. The principle behind the method is that by enriching a job, the individual increases his or her job satisfaction and thus experiences motivation that the organization considers positive. Vertical job enrichment adds more authority, accountability, degree of difficulty and specialization to an individual's work. By doing so, motivational factors such as responsibility, achievement, advancement, recognition, growth, and learning are further developed.

Job rotation is the movement between different jobs in order to increase interest and motivation. One day, a person may be working in one part of the factory, and the next day, they may work in a different part. The advantage of this rotation is it helps employees avoid boredom because they are doing different jobs all the time and learning new skills. Job rotation is similar to job enlargement in that it widens the activities of a worker by switching him or her around a range of work.

Participative management

Participative management is the idea of utilizing the knowledge, strengths, creativity and ingenuity of all employees within an organization and not simply relying on the managers and supervisors to direct work. With

participative management, companies are asking workers, in groups and teams, to get involved in making suggestions, setting goals, improving methods, solving problems, and enhancing the quality of the company's products and services. The goal of participative management is to create high-performance teams capable of managing their own operating routines. It is based on the belief that both the company and its people benefit when managers and employees actively participate in decisions that affect them and their organization.

The common benefits that are proponents of participative management include:

- Better communication and greater employee involvement
- Improved effectiveness and increased productivity
- Empowered staff that is more able to offer practical solutions
- More positive work environment
- Renewed sense of pride and ownership for all staff

Participative management is a synthesis of several management theories, and the basic principle of this management model is that it requires participation from all of the employees and managers to actively pursue a common goal.

Performance-based pay

This management method seeks to enhance employee motivation and productivity by sharing the financial results of enterprise performance with employees. In essence, performance pay is based on paying the worker for his or her unique value, rather than assessing a value to the job itself. Such schemes fall into four broad categories:

- **Individual**: based on individual performance, such as incentive schemes and sales commissions

- **Profit-sharing:** applies to all or most of the employees

- **Gain sharing:** measured by a pre-determined performance formula, applicable to all or groups of employees. The performance measure may be profit or some other objective such as productivity

- **Employees**: share ownership schemes

Gain sharing divides the results of improved performance between the employer and employees. If a department increases productivity over a certain period, then a percentage of that increased productivity is attributed to company gains and is shared among employees. The assumption is that the better use of human resources results in improved performance, and the productivity gains are then shared with those responsible: the employees. The gains are typically distributed according to an agreed, pre-determined formula. The system works on the premise that by linking a part of earnings to productivity, the employees will respond by increasing their labor productivity.

The gain sharing component of an employee's compensation is paid in the form of a bonus and therefore demonstrates a direct linkage between the employee's performance and the compensation earned.

Profit sharing systems are not related to an individual's performance, but are linked to the profits of an enterprise. The direct relationship between individual performance and company performance is less obvious but the aim is usually to demonstrate the power of teamwork within the company. Here again, the profit is split with employees according to some predetermined formula.

Long-term incentive plans are operated, especially for executives, both as an incentive to improve performance and in order to reduce fixed costs. Examples of such schemes are:

- **Share option plans** promote convergence of stockholder/executive interests.

- **Bonus pay** is linked to long-term performance (3-5 years) to encourage a focus on long-term goals.

These incentives are quite common in large, publicly owned corporations and can result in enormous take-home earnings when executives decide to cash in. When money is a strong motivator for an individual, these programs can be quite effective, and they are economically sound especially when an industry is experiencing a downturn.

A **performance bonus** can be based on individual or group performance. When it is individual-based, the payment depends on performance ratings; group-based bonuses are dependent upon team performance ratings. The overall management of this type of bonus system is extremely important, as there is ample room for claims of favoritism due to the subjectivity of the process.

Skill-based pay refers to a pay system in which pay increases are linked to the number or depth of skills an employee applies to his or her job. This method is used as a means of developing broader and deeper skills among the workforce. Such increases are given in addition to, and not in lieu of, general pay increases employees may receive. The pay increases are usually tied to three types of skills:

- **Horizontal skills:** involves a broadening of skills in terms of the range of tasks
- **Vertical skills:** involves acquiring skills of a higher level
- **Depth skills:** involves a high level of skills in specialized areas relating to the same job.

Skill-based pay rewards a person for what he or she is worth to the organization, not what his or her job is worth to the organization. It takes into consideration that each employee brings a different set of skills and knowledge to a position, and therefore, the total contribution to the organization will change depending on who is doing what. This system encourages flexibility, skill development, and continuous learning.

A **self-directed work team** is a group of people who combine different skills and talents to work toward a common purpose or goal. Members of a self-directed work team are involved on a routine basis in decision-making, goal setting, scheduling, hiring, planning, peer review, and problem solving. They use their company's mission statement to develop their purpose and direct their activity. Because a manager or boss does not necessarily lead the tea, they must agree on the rules and deadlines for accomplishing what they set out to do. Many do this through the creation of a charter. If problems arise during the course of a project, the team members work together to provide a solution.

The role of managers and supervisors within organizations that support self-directed teams is to help develop the team's self-directive capabilities. Rather than control and direct, the supervisors facilitate skill development. They also manage the interactions among other self-directed work teams in the organization.

The notion behind self-directed work teams is maximizing employees' capabilities to contribute to organizational performance fosters an extremely high level of employee commitment. It is also linked to efforts to improve leadership and management skills among all employees.

All of these management methods have distinct merits and deserve careful consideration within organizations today. The issue at the heart of creating motivation-rich workplaces is that none of these methods alone, or in combination, will motivate all employees at all times. You can experiment with any or all of these methods, and you will find that some managers  respond well to some systems, as do the employees themselves. But it is only when you view the management method as one aspect of employee motivation that you will truly see an improvement in what we deem positive employee motivation levels.

The Management

As we have been discussing throughout this book, different people have different internal motivating factors that influence how they react to the work they do. The internal motivators operating within an organization's managers have as great an affect on productivity as what is influencing their subordinate's behavior. It's the manager who has the greatest influence, and if the manager is not "buying into" the management method of the day, then he or she will be ineffective in using and applying the principles needed for the best outcome.

Every manager comes to his or her job with strong beliefs, values, and motivating principles. If the management method espoused by the organization is not congruent with those beliefs, values, and principles, then the manager suffers an internal conflict. He or she has to fight against his or her natural tendencies and ascribe to a way of dealing with people, directing work, and making decisions that just do not fit. Then, the manager's department performance is threatened when the organization's policies and managerial practices are out of sync with his or her beliefs..

When productivity, morale, or other issues surface within that manager's department, the traditional answer to the problem is to send the manager on a training course. The thought is that by further educating the manager on the tools and techniques specific to a particular management method, the manager will change his or her management behavior and beliefs. This indoctrination, so to speak, is often less than satisfactory, and while the manager may show some "improvement" in the short term, his or her natural style will eventually creep back in.

The whole notion of fitting a manager to a method rather than finding a method that fits the manager is flawed. This solution is based on the erroneous belief that there is one best way to manage people and that the "best" way just happens to be the management method that is currently being used. I'm hoping you're beginning to agree that this is an ineffective premise to base a solution upon. **Trying to fit a manager to a certain mold is often like trying to fit a square peg into a round hole: it causes frustration for the person trying to make the fit and severe discomfort for the person trying to be fit.**

When organizations encourage and facilitate incongruence between a manager and the method under which he or she must manage, the resulting performance is mediocre at best and a dismal failure at worst. The repercussions of ineffective management are then felt throughout the department and organization as the manager's employees are left without effective leadership, direction, or support.

The Managed

Following the same arguments as above, when the practices of management are out of sync with the way the employee wants to be supervised, then the performance of him or her suffers. Here again, we are talking about the fact that not all people will respond positively to one particular method of management. Some employees will look at participative management as an ideal way to grow professionally and contribute meaningfully to the organization as a whole. Others will see it as demanding and invasive, requiring them to act outside their comfort zone.

Those espousing participative management will respond that pushing people to explore their potential is a good thing and that both the organization and individual will benefit in the long run. This is a noble undertaking, but what effect does it have on the employee who is being forced to behave in a way that is unnatural and unwelcome? It will definitely cause undue stress and discomfort, which are two major, contributing factors to employee dissatisfaction. A dissatisfied employee is motivated all right — motivated to run in the opposite direction and hope for a change in management regimes. Now, the manager has a great employee who is plummeting in job performance because of management methods.

Approaching motivational strategies with a one-prescription approach ignores the internal motivation factors that operate differently within each person.

In order to develop a motivation-rich environment, you must consider each individual who is a part of your organization and the ways he or she responds to motivating stimuli.

The Work

The final factor that needs to be considered when designing a motivation-rich work environment is the actual work that needs to be done within the organization. When the methods for managing are incongruent with the work to be done, then the performance of the work is negatively affected. When the work is highly structured and routinized, adding complicated layers of management hampers

rather than helps productivity. When you don't require a team of people to decide how best to screw in a light bulb, don't use one. When a job can be redesigned for maximum satisfaction, consider the possibility.

The point here is that just as there is no one "right" way to manage, neither is there one "right" way to organize jobs. The emphasis is again on making the job fit the people and the managerial techniques. Job design is a complicated subject, but it deserves some attention.

The following is a summary of one technique you can apply within your organization. This introduction will give you some basic tools and the confidence you need to begin looking at the work structures you currently use.

Job Design: The Job Characteristics Model

When we talk about the work that is done within organizations, there is a very useful framework that allows us to analyze and design jobs. It's called the Job Characteristics Model, and it describes every job in terms of the following five core job dimensions:

Skill variety: the degree to which a job requires a variety of activities so the worker can use a number of different skills and talents.

Task identity: the degree to which the job requires completion of a whole and identifiable piece of work.

Task significance: the degree to which the job has a substantial impact on the lives or work of other people.

Autonomy: the degree to which the job provides substantial freedom, independence, and discretion to the individuals in scheduling work and in determining the procedures to be used in carrying out the tasks.

Feedback: the degree to which carrying out the work activities required by the job results in the individual obtaining direct and clear information about the effectiveness of his or her performance.

The first three dimensions — skill variety, task identity, and task significance — combine to create meaningful work. If these three characteristics exist in a job, we can predict that the person will view the job as being important, valuable, and worthwhile. A job that allows autonomy gives the worker a sense of personal responsibility for the results, and if the job provides feedback, the employee will know how effectively he or she is performing. From a motivational standpoint, the Job Characteristics Model says that an employee obtains internal rewards when that person knows he or she personally has performed well on a task that he or she cares about.

Jobs high in motivating potential must be high in at least one of the three factors so employees experience something meaningful at work, plus they must be high on both autonomy and feedback. If jobs score high on motivating potential, the Job Characteristics Model predicts that motivation, performance, and satisfaction will be positively affected, while the likelihood of absence and turnover is lessened. What managers can learn from the Job Characteristics Model are specific ways to make changes to jobs that will most likely increase the motivational factors within each job.

Combine tasks. Wherever possible, managers should take tasks that were split apart in the name of efficiency and put them back together to form new, larger modules of work that will increase skill variety and task identity.

Create natural work units. The creation of natural work units means the tasks employees do form an identifiable and meaningful whole. This increases employee ownership of the work and improves the likelihood that employees will view their work as meaningful and important rather than as irrelevant and boring.

Establish client relationships. The client is the end user of the product or service the employee works on. Wherever possible, the manager should try to establish direct relationships between workers and their clients. This will increase skill variety, autonomy, and feedback opportunities for the employee. The opportunity for increased awareness of the impact of one's work on others is a powerful motivator.

Expand jobs vertically. Vertical expansion gives employees responsibilities and controls that were formally reserved for management. It seeks to partially close the gap between the doing and the controlling aspects of the job and increases employee autonomy.

Open feedback channels. By increasing feedback, employees not only learn how well they are performing their jobs, but also whether their performance is improving, deteriorating, or remaining at a constant level. Ideally, this feedback about performance should be received directly as the employee does the job rather than from management on an occasional or even periodic basis.

The Job Characteristics Model is one way to determine the type of intrinsic motivational factors contained within a job. When discussing the type of work an employee is doing, it is a valuable exercise to examine ways the work can be reorganized to suit individual needs and desires.

The way work is managed is an important factor for employee success, and you want to make the process as simple and straightforward as possible. The more hoops that people need to jump through, the more opportunity for dissatisfaction; the less satisfied employees are, the less motivated they are to do a good job. It is imperative that you not choose management systems simply because they are considered the latest and greatest. Just as certain management systems work for certain people, some systems work only for some types of work and not for others.

The only way to achieve an environment that motivates all employees in the direction your organization desires is to align the four factors we have been discussing:

- Management Method
- The Managed
- The Manager
- The Work

Without congruity within these subsystems, you will never have a workplace that is totally dedicated to meeting your organizational needs and working at peak-performance levels.

Four Workplace Organization Rules

Based on the concept of the four interrelated work factors and our discussion about how these factors influence the way a workplace needs to be managed, we can develop four rules for workplace organization.

1. Different work must be organized in different ways.

2. The natural, personal style of the manager must fit with the work being done and the people who are doing the work.

3. Employee values, beliefs, and principles must be compatible with the way they are being managed and the work they are doing.

4. The particular managerial principles utilized by the manager must fit with the work to be done, the person doing the work, and the manager's style of managing.

Following these four rules creates a large degree of complexity within workplaces, but humans are complex beings, and there are no short cuts — especially when it comes to optimizing motivation and performance. It really is not as difficult as it appears. The key is to commit yourself to the premise that there is no one "right" way to manage. Once you remove this main obstacle, you will begin to see all of the employees within your organization as unique individuals who bring their own capabilities, values, and beliefs to the workplace. When you recognize that none of these people are unmotivated or "wrong," you will be able to tackle the issue of employee motivation from an individual perspective; this is when your workplace transformation will take place.

Example: Keys Manufacturing

Keys Manufacturing produces Hoozits. The process to produce a Hoozit involves fabricating and combining three different parts: the wheely, the rotator, and the pin. Keys Manufacturing has three separate production departments each headed by a manager, and these managers all have different natural management styles. Bob, who is in charge of the fabrication of Wheelies, is an authoritative manager who has been with the company for 20 years and runs a tight ship. Fred, who is in charge of producing the rotators and affixing the pins in preparation for the final assembly process, is a new graduate from a progressive business school. He is very into the team approach and equality management. Gayle, the manager of the third production department, oversees the final assembly of the wheely to the rotator and pin combination. She is a real people person who likes to foster personal relationships with her employees and has been working at Keys Manufacturing for five years.

Keys Manufacturing has been struggling with poor productivity and what seems to be a low level of motivation within the three production departments for the last two quarters — from around the same time that Fred joined the management team. Prior to Fred's arrival, there were only two production departments. Productivity was high, but it was hampered by an inefficient system. That is what prompted the decision to split production into three stages and hire a third manager.

When Taylor, the operations manager, assessed the situation, he applied the principles for creating a congruent workforce and realized that after the reshuffle, each manager had people under him who were operating under three different behavioral and belief systems. Before the shuffle, most of the employee/manager incongruence had been attended to, but in the name of efficiency, those changes were discarded and staff members were assigned to a department based on skills and experience alone.

What Taylor did to address the problem was reorganize the departments based on the kind of work being done and the suitability of the manager's natural style to the management style an employee responded to best. Then, within each department, the manager assigned duties based on each employee's preferences, natural ability, and aptitude. The process was time consuming and the restructure caused an initial productivity decrease due to retraining requirements, but within three months, the morale, satisfaction, and productivity had climbed to levels that exceeded everyone's expectations. The managers were able to lead effectively using techniques that came naturally to them, and the employees were performing work and being managed in ways that best suited them.

This very simplified example gives you an idea of what it means to reorganize an entire workplace based on the four rules of workplace congruence. In the real world, the solutions will not be so neat and straightforward, but the end rewards should be as significant. I didn't say it was easy, but with the right motivation and commitment on your part, it is doable.

To accomplish the task of creating a congruent workplace means putting employee's needs first. It also necessitates getting to know your employees and developing a true understanding of what makes them tick. It's not enough to know that Joe works in accounting; you need to take the time to know what makes Joe in accounting unique, what he values, what he likes about his job, what he dislikes about his job, and what he believes is an effective management system. Once you have the answers to these questions, you will know how the company can bring out the best in him, and then it is your responsibility to make that happen.

The process of creating workplace congruence starts with open communication and includes systems that allow every employee to indicate the kind of work they are comfortable with, the type of management style they prefer, and one where managers can indicate their natural management style preferences.

Hiring Criteria

The most practical approach to creating congruence within your company is to develop hiring criteria based on the four factors required for workplace congruence. In other words, hire for cultural fit. Your culture is the outward manifestation of your corporate values, beliefs and principles, and the leaders, managers, and supervisors within your organization most often represent this culture. The employees you bring into your business must support and nurture that culture, which they do by contributing positively to daily interactions and ultimately finding their own success and fulfillment. Within a culture that motivates, you will find employees doing work they enjoy for bosses they relate to.

When you start with the right employees in the right positions, you are proactively addressing the ultimate motivation question: "How should Manager X manage Employee Y to do Z? To determine if a job candidate can be effectively managed by Manager X to do whatever the position requires, your need to take the time to find out who your candidates really are. You have to get beyond the education and experiences listed on their resume and find out what brings out the best in that person.

Ask questions in the interview process that address the "fit" factor and that reveal important information related to motivation, preferences, beliefs, and values. Here are some questions to use as guidelines:

1. Tell me about the best boss you ever worked for. What made the relationship effective?

2. Tell me about a time when you were most dissatisfied working with a manager. What exactly caused the dissatisfaction?

3. Recall for me a time when you found it very difficult to get along with a coworker. What was the root of the problem?

4. If you could create the ideal work environment, what would it be like?

5. When were you most satisfied with your work performance?

6. What is the best thing a boss has ever said to you?

7. Tell me about a time when you were unmotivated and someone at your workplace was able to help you out of your slump. What did he or she do or say?

8. What is the most discouraging thing a boss has ever done or said to you? Why?

9. What is the best reward you have ever received at work?

10. What do you know about our company that excites you?

As you can see, all of these questions are designed to get the candidate thinking and talking about what is important to them and what makes a constructive, positive work environment. Your job is to evaluate how well your current environment, the work you offer, and the style of the management available will motivate the candidate to do a good, if not exceptional, job.

As we have been discussing, it is difficult for people to fight against their personality and natural inclinations, and it is next to impossible to mold someone to fit into a situation where their values and principles are not inline with the environment. Start your employees off on a positive motivational track by making selection choices that enhance their natural motivation: you and your employees will be much more satisfied.

Planned Job Placement

This method is one that organizations with existing motivation and performance issues will need to apply. The process is similar to recruitment where you are starting from scratch with current employees to determine where, within your company, each one will get the most out of the work relationship.

You can accomplish this through informal meetings and conversations with staff, surveys and questionnaires that you design yourself, or there are a wide variety of tests available which are designed to uncover personality, interests, aptitudes, and management style preferences. The following are sample questionnaires you can use with your employees to uncover their underlying motivational factors, their current motivation level, and how they approach motivating others.

Questionnaire #1: MOTIVATIONAL FACTORS

General Instructions

Answer honestly: There are no right or wrong answers. Your answers reflect your individuality, and that is what we are trying to uncover.

Be specific: When asked for examples, please provide as much detail as possible. The more we know about your unique set of skills, values, and preferences, the higher the chance for a successful match.

Be introspective: Take your time to answer the questions from your core beliefs, values, ideals, principles, etc. The more in-tune you are with what you truly desire from work, the better able we are to provide a fulfilling work environment.

Remember: this is not a test — there is no pass or fail. This is simply the best way for us to determine "fit."

Questions

1. When people meet you for the first time, what about their first impression is most inaccurate? (*This uncovers what the person values versus what they believe society values. The incongruence is important in that you get insight into how they might "try" to behave or come across vs. how they will truly perform.*)

2. Describe the workplace where you achieved the most satisfaction. Discuss specifically what makes that workplace stand out from the rest.

3. Describe the workplace where you were the least satisfied. Discuss specifically the cause of your dissatisfaction.

4. If you could create the ideal workplace, what would it look like?

5. What has been your greatest work-related achievement? Please provide details about the job and the workplace where this achievement occurred. (*You're looking for a link between high performance and work environment — the ideal answer is one that occurred at the workplace described in question No. 2.*)

6. Your ideal work hours are:

   ☐ Monday to Friday; 9-5
   ☐ Flexible work time; 8 hour days
   ☐ No rules, I have a job to do and I take as many hours as needed to do it
   ☐ Other: _____

7. Your ideal remuneration is:

   ☐ Hourly pay
   ☐ Fixed salary
   ☐ Salary with a performance component
   ☐ Complete performance-based pay

8. What is your expectation for yearly earnings?
   - ☐ Less than $30,000
   - ☐ $30K to $50K
   - ☐ $50K to 75K
   - ☐ More than $75K
   - ☐ Money is not an expectation for me

9. What is the best reward (monetary or otherwise) you have ever received at work? What made it so valuable to you?

Questions 10 to 16 are interrelated, please answer as such.

10. If you had no limitations (geographical, type of industry, remuneration, etc.), what organization would you work for?

11. Again, with no limitations (education, experience, specific skills, etc.), what function would you be performing in that organization?

12. In that function, what are the key responsibilities you would have?

13. What are the main differences between that "ideal" role and the role you currently fulfill in your organization? (You are looking for major differences between experience and desire — it indicates where true passion lies.)

14. What is holding you back from pursuing/getting your ideal role?

15. Given what you know about our company, what is your ideal role here?

16. What job title would best describe your ideal role? (You are looking for creativity and unconventionality.)

17. What type of people do you prefer to work with?

18. Tell me about the most difficult coworker you ever worked with. What about the situation was most frustrating, and what was the outcome?

19. When making a decision you:

- [ ] Go with your gut.
- [ ] Observe what has been done in the past, what was considered right.
- [ ] Make quick decisions that deal with the here and now.
- [ ] Consult superiors for advice and guidance.
- [ ] Look toward the future and strategize.
- [ ] Involve many others and seek consensus/ cooperation.
- [ ] Integrate many perspectives and stretch your thinking.
- [ ] Examine how others would make the decision and decide based on a holistic view of the world.

20. You work because:

- [ ] You need to earn a living.
- [ ] Work provides security.
- [ ] You need to be doing something.
- [ ] That is what responsible adults do.
- [ ] You are achievement and success oriented.
- [ ] You desire to make a positive contribution to the world.
- [ ] You value continual learning and self-improvement.
- [ ] You want to change the world.

21. Which of the following people would you <u>most</u> want to work with?

- [ ] Someone with the same background and same outlook on life
- [ ] Someone with different experiences who has come to see the world the way you see it
- [ ] Someone who is open to new ideas
- [ ] Someone who sees the world totally different than you
- [ ] Someone who has an entirely different cultural background

22. Which of the following people would you <u>least</u> want to work with?

☐ Someone with the same background and same outlook on life

☐ Someone with different experiences who has come to see the world the way you see it

☐ Someone who promotes new ideas

☐ Someone who sees the world totally different than you

☐ Someone who has an entirely different cultural background

23. What is your perspective on a hierarchical work structure?

☐ It indicates your value within the company.

☐ That is how work evolved, and it seems to be working.

☐ It is often the only way to see to it that people do what they are supposed to do.

☐ I appreciate having superiors; I like order and structure.

☐ It is an efficient way to define strategies, determine what needs to be done, and achieve goals.

☐ It impedes effective communication within the organization.

☐ It places people into limiting roles and hampers full development.

☐ It is completely unnecessary; organizations consist of people already working toward a common goal, so they don't need any limiting forces.

24. What about our company excites you?

Questionnaire #2: Current Motivation and Performance Assessment

General Instructions

Answer honestly: There are no right or wrong answers. Your answers reflect your individuality, and that is what we are trying to uncover.

Be specific: When asked for examples, please provide as much detail as possible. The more we know about your unique set of skills, values, and preferences, the higher the chance for a successful match.

Be introspective: Take your time to answer the questions from your core beliefs, values, ideals, principles, etc. The more in-tune you are with what you truly desire from work, the better able we are to provide a fulfilling work environment.

Remember: this is not a test — there is no pass or fail. This is simply the best way for us to determine "fit."

Use the following key.

Rating Scale

1. Strongly Disagree
2. Disagree
3. Neutral
4. Agree
5. Strongly Agree

Rate the following statements on a 1-5 scale using the Rating Scale. Apply the questions to your current work situation.

- ☐ My manager and I would assess my work performance similarly.
- ☐ I have received adequate training to perform the duties of my assigned job.
- ☐ I believe my skills and aptitudes are well suited to my current job responsibilities.

☐ I am provided the necessary supplies and resources needed to perform my job well.

☐ My manager sets clear and reasonable expectations for my performance.

☐ Rewards are distributed equally within my department and are given based on performance.

☐ The rewards available to me hold personal value and are worth striving for.

☐ I feel I am doing a good job, but my manager has given me feedback to the contrary.

☐ If I had more training, my performance would greatly improve.

☐ The job I am doing is too difficult for my current skill level.

☐ I believe that if I had access to appropriate supplies and resources, my work performance would improve.

☐ My manager makes unrealistic demands, and I never know what is expected of me.

☐ My manager has favorites within the department, and they are rewarded unfairly.

☐ The rewards available to me within this company have little or no personal value.

Now, score your assessment.

Step 1:

- For each question with a "reverse" scoring, the value of your response is 6 minus your rating value.

- For each question with a "regular" scoring, the value of your response equals your rating value.

Question	Scoring	Value	Question	Scoring	Value
1	Reverse	_____	8	Regular	_____
2	Reverse	_____	9	Regular	_____
3	Reverse	_____	10	Regular	_____
4	Reverse	_____	11	Regular	_____
5	Reverse	_____	12	Regular	_____
6	Reverse	_____	13	Regular	_____
7	Reverse	_____	14	Regular	_____

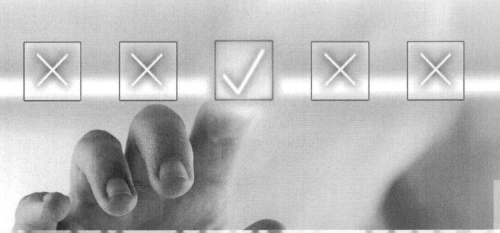

Step 2:

Combine your scores for each performance/motivation issue

Issue	Score per Question		Total
Perception of Performance	1. _____	8. _____	_____
Training Provided	2. _____	9. _____	_____
Aptitude	3. _____	10. _____	_____
Resources Supplied	4. _____	11. _____	_____
Expectations	5. _____	12. _____	_____
Incentives	6. _____	13. _____	_____
Reward Value	7. _____	14. _____	_____
		Total Score	

- Scores greater than seven for any performance/motivation issue indicates a problem that needs to be addressed.
- Total scores over 50 indicate a broad-based motivational deficiency.

Assessing Performance and Motivating Others

General Instructions

Answer honestly: There are no right or wrong answers. Your answers reflect your individuality and that is what we are trying to uncover.

Be specific: When asked for examples please provide as much detail as possible. The more we know about your unique set of skills, values, and preferences the higher the chance for a successful match.

Be Introspective: Take your time to answer the questions from your core beliefs, values, ideals, principles, etc... The more in-tune you are with what you truly desire from work, the better able we are to provide a fulfilling work environment.

Remember this is not a test – there is no pass or fail. This is simply the best way for us to determine "fit."

Questionnaire #3: Motivating Others and Performance Assessment

Use the following key.

Rating Scale

1. Strongly Disagree
2. Disagree
3. Slightly Disagree
4. Slightly Agree
5. Agree
6. Strongly Agree

Rate the following statements on a 1-6 scale using the Rating Scale.

When dealing with a performance or motivation issue I:

☐ Approach the problem by identifying whether the issue is caused by lack of motivation or ability.

☐ Establish a clear standard of performance.

☐ Offer to provide training and support as required but I do not complete the assignment myself.

☐ Provide honest and straightforward feedback regarding the performance and potential consequences.

☐ Have a variety of reward methods to choose from when recognizing good performance.

- ☐ I take appropriate disciplinary actions making sure to provide specific suggestion for improvement.

- ☐ Design tasks to ensure they are interesting and challenging.

- ☐ Strive to provide rewards that are valued.

- ☐ Treat people fairly and equitably.

- ☐ Provide timely feedback for everyone and ensure feedback is provided from relevant coworkers as well.

- ☐ Take time to analyze the performance issue before taking remedial or disciplinary action.

- ☐ Assist people with establishing performance goals that are SMART (specific, measurable, appropriate, realistic, and time-bound).

- ☐ View termination as a last resort for any performance issue.

- ☐ Link rewards to high performance wherever applicable.

- ☐ Fairly and consistently apply discipline for performance that is below capability and expectations.

- ☐ Use job enrichment to expose people to a variety of tasks and skills.

- ☐ Arrange for appropriate uses of teamwork.

- ☐ Make sure people are using realistic measures when judging my fairness.

- ☐ Immediately provide positive feedback and recognition for significant accomplishments.

- ☐ Ensure people have the resources and support necessary to perform at or above expectations.

Copy the scores in the following chart.

Skill	Question/Score
Identifying performance issues	1. _____ 11. _____
Establishing clear expectations and goal setting	2. _____ 12. _____
Supporting and enhancing performance	3. _____ 13. _____ 20. _____
Linking performance to rewards and discipline	5. _____ 14. _____ 6. _____ 15. _____
Using incentives that have value	7. _____ 16. _____ 8. _____ 17. _____
Distributing rewards fairly and equitably	9. _____ 18. _____
Providing timely and honest feedback	4. _____ 10. _____ 19. _____
Total Score	

To find out how well you assess performance and motivate others, compare your total score to the following data. (Maximum score is 120)

≥101	Top Quartile
94-100	Second Quartile
85-93	Third Quartile
≤ 84	Bottom Quartile

When you gather information from all of your employees regarding their beliefs, practices, aptitudes, and interests, you can begin the process of matching and work reorganization where necessary. Use the answers to the survey questions or the test results to begin a dialogue with your employees and to discover more about each one as an individual. This depth of knowledge and understanding will assist immeasurably in creating a congruent workplace and facilitating a motivation-rich work environment for everyone.

Ineffective performance arises when we don't know how Manager X should lead Employee Y to do Z. The most effective and thorough way to address that fundamental motivation question is through creating congruence between the four factors that lead to employee satisfaction and success: management methods, the manager, the managed, and the work. When performance problems arise, they can often be attributed to the fact that in any organization, in any department, we find work requiring a basic kind of producer being done by people with many different beliefs and values who want to be managed in ways different than the natural style of the manager.

Extensive evaluation and analysis of each employee's needs, desires, and internal motivators is the key to discovering how best to use the talent you currently employ so they can all be engaged in meaningful and satisfying work. The end result of a workplace full of satisfied and fulfilled employees is an environment where motivation flourishes, productivity is at or near capacity, and organizational success is optimized.

Now that you have a solid grasp on how to build a motivation-rich foundation, we need to discuss the next steps in sustaining a motivation-rich environment over the long term. As you know now, employee motivation is subject to continual change, which means that your work with motivation is one that requires diligent effort on a continual basis. To build a strong motivation culture, you need to commit to reevaluating your efforts and building processes that are inherently motivating to all of your employees.

The main factor in a sustainable, motivating workplace is employee recognition — and not gimmicky or showy recognition, but true appreciation and gratitude for a job well done. You may think you have a great recognition program in place or that you recognize employee's efforts already, but please read the next chapter and think critically about what it is you recognize, how you recognize it, and how it is truly perceived by others within your organization.

Chapter 4

Understanding Employee Recognition

Recognition is critical in motivating, satisfying, and retaining employees.

Praise and recognition are essential building blocks of a great workplace. All people possess the need to be recognized as individuals and to feel a sense of accomplishment. Recognition is an external motivator that applies to everyone. While there is nothing complicated about recognition, it is one of the items that most employees cite as missing from their workplaces.

A prevalent attitude in today's society is the notion that in order to do a good job and achieve our work related goals we must be very task- and goal-oriented. At work, the high (even medium) achievers seem so driven and focused. They are rushing here and rushing there, tending to issues, putting out fires, fielding requests… the priority is anything that is directly related to task achievement. When this occurs, what tends to happen is that people at work forget that there are lots of other people at work and that relationships with those people are a necessary component for success.

Recognition isn't something you "do" like all the other tasks you have at work. Recognition is a mindset; it is a way of relating to your employees on a daily basis. You are never "done" recognizing, and it never gets checked off your to-do list. When you commit to recognition, you must commit to treating your employees as people. It's simple, but it takes a reframing of the purpose of your interactions with everyone at work.

The small interactions that occur on a regular basis are what make a real impact on employees. You do this when you praise someone, when you hold team meetings, when you keep your staff informed about changes, when you express confidence in someone's ability, and even when you give someone a warm smile. **You are communicating that you recognize the importance and value of others** and therein lays the motivating power of recognition.

"Recognition is so easy to do and so inexpensive to distribute that there is simply no excuse for not doing it."

-Rosabeth Moss Kanter,
Author and Harvard Business School Professor

Recognition—A Worthy Challenge

One element common to all individuals is the need for reward and praise. It is something we work hard for and yet, all too often, our work goes unrecognized. We do a good job, we get results, but somehow, we don't get thanked. Why is this? In too many cases, the notion of recognition has been overanalyzed. We have made the process so complex and full of rules when, in fact, it is very simple.

- Thank employees for a job well done
- Be appreciative
- Acknowledge good work

There is nothing more motivating than praise and recognition. At the root of every effective workplace performance program is a philosophy of recognizing and appreciating employees. To quote Bob Nelson, the motivation mastermind, "You get the best effort from others not by lighting a fire beneath them, but by building a fire within them." This is where the power of reward and recognition becomes so powerful and so undeniable. **By recognizing an employee's work, you are providing intrinsic motivation for him to do better and be better.**

If you are still thinking of recognition as another complication to your already hectic job, think again. Recognition doesn't need to be time consuming or complex, and the results of meaningful recognition will significantly reduce the other stressors you have in your work life that are caused by dissatisfied employees.

With effective recognition, you will find that employees are more willing to get involved with problem solving, and they will rely less on you to find the solutions. The more appreciated an employee feels, the more connected he or she feels to the work. This increased connectivity leads to increased pride and ownership and a desire to take on more responsibility. As employees are more committed to their work, they will show an increased concern for quality and company reputation. Their increased investment in the company is a direct result of meaningful recognition, and they will naturally want to contribute more to the workplace — even in the face of adversity.

If you are still in doubt, take a look at the results of a Recognition-Performance survey conducted by Bob Nelson, considered one of the leading experts on workplace motivation:

STATEMENT	AGREEMENT
"Recognizing employees helps me better motivate them."	90.5%
"Providing non-monetary recognition to my employees when they do good work helps to increase their performance."	84.4%
"Recognizing employees provides them with practical feedback."	84.4%
"Recognizing my employees for good work makes it easier to get the work done."	80.3%
"Recognizing employees helps them to be more productive."	77.7%
"Providing non-monetary recognition helps me to achieve my personal goals."	69.3%
"Providing non-monetary recognition helps me to achieve my job goals."	60.3%

- 72.9% of managers reported that they received the results they expected when they used recognition either immediately or soon after the event being recognized occurred.

- 98.8% of managers said they felt they would eventually obtain the desired results by using recognition.

- 77.6 % of the employees who worked for the managers participating in the survey said that it was very or extremely important to be recognized by their manager when they do good work.

- The time frame that these same employees expected recognition to occur after the event was:
  - Immediately (20%)
  - Soon thereafter (52.9%)
  - Sometime later (18.8%)

These results support the dynamic and self-reinforcing effect of recognition in the workplace as follows:

1. A manager using recognition is reinforced by the impact that the recognition has on improving employee's job performance.

2. Improved employee performance reinforces the manager to continue providing recognition.

Effective recognition breathes life into a workplace. It creates a dynamic exchange of ideas, and it boosts morale, productivity, loyalty, and motivation. These qualities will make your job as a manager much easier, and you will wonder why you ever griped about having to recognize people in the first place.

Recognition That Works

> "This business of making another person feel good in the unspectacular course of his/her daily comings and goings is, in my view, the very essence of leadership."
>
> *-Irwin Federman*
> CEO Monolithic Memories, Inc.

To understand the difference between recognition that works and recognition that doesn't, I want you to recall the story I related about my own experiences with workplace motivation and recognition at the beginning of this book. Remember: we had put in numerous programs designed to recognize and reward employees, but none of them actually worked. Well, here are some comments from employees in other organizations that support why those programs were dismal failures:

- "Please, not another golf shirt!"

- "Why spend money on all these silly trinkets? Put the money to use and buy us a photocopier that prints more than 5 pages a minute."

- "Think of the trees and time wasted printing those crazy certificates. What do we do with them? Take them home and display them on the fridge?"

- "If I have to spend another lunch hour listening to the employee of the month speech, I'm gonna lose it."

- "Rather than go through some big hoopla, why not just tell us when we do something well?"

Do you recognize your own recognition efforts in any of those comments? It's easy to fall into the trap of meaningless recognition, because it takes little to no personal involvement. The recognition programs alluded to in the above comments are all company sponsored. As a manager or supervisor, you don't really contribute anything to the process. The very items that we have been trained to consider as recognition have very little recognition value. We too often equate reward with recognition, and while the reward may be nice to have when its in the form of a raise, bonus, plaque, or prize, it's the thought behind the reward that is the actual recognition and that is exactly what gets lost in the giving.

For rewards to count as recognition, employees need to see acknowledgment of their specific accomplishments and sincere appreciation for their personal value to the organization. Without that link, a reward is just another external motivator that may or may not have value to the individual receiving it. This doesn't mean, however, that there is no place for reward in the workplace. Rewards can be very motivating (providing it has value to the person receiving it), and it is important to think of new and creative ways to execute them. The point you need to remember is that the reward itself does not equal recognition.

You can make a reward a form of recognition by delivering the reward in such a way that fosters recognition. Perks, incentives, and bonuses themselves aren't recognition, but by personalizing them, the employee then perceives it as a form of recognition. Rather than handing out bonus checks with the regular payroll, meet employees and tell them how the company did, stress that everyone's hard work contributed to the prosperity, and that the company is appreciative of their efforts.

When an incentive is earned, make sure you meet with the employee directly and discuss what he or she did that directly contributed to the receipt of the incentive. Do the same for perks, plaques, and other rewards that are given periodically. The key is to tie the reward to employee performance and then express appreciation.

Six Factors of Effective Recognition

Effective recognition can be defined as, "Motivation that increases the self-esteem and initiative of the recipient, resulting in a lasting improvement in their behavior and performance, which positively impacts the bottom line." When expressing appreciation and recognizing employees, you must take into consideration the following six basic factors of effective recognition.

Recognition that motivates is:

- **Genuine**: It is not forced, and it has no ulterior motive.
- **Spontaneous**: It is not premeditated, planned, or prepared.
- **Personal**: It means something special to the person it is given to and he or she is singled out for praise.
- **Specific**: It is more than "good job" or "way to go;" it's a thank you or acknowledgement for something specific that was done.
- **Timely**: It comes as close to the event as possible — this reinforces spontaneity.
- **Public**: Expressing thanks is generally not a "behind closed doors" event. Find ways to let everyone know how proud you are of the work that is being done. **Note: For those individuals who you know are uncomfortable with high visibility, do not publicly acknowledge — this will only end up embarrassing and de-motivating him or her.

Not all six factors have to be present for recognition to be important, but you need to aim for as many as possible every time. The only exception is the notion of public praise — some people are very averse to publicity, and the embarrassment of the situation will take away any recognition value. Remember: your goal is to relate to your employees in meaningful terms, and through your understanding and relationship with your employees, you will know whether public praise is appropriate or not.

Recognition opportunities are everywhere. Employees are looking for proof that they are valued and appreciated in everything you do and everything you say. That means you have to make recognition an inherent part of your work environment. From the amount and type of information you communicate, to the trust you demonstrate, to the safety of your workplace; every opportunity for interaction with employees is an opportunity to convey appreciation and value.

Build a Recognition Culture

Recognition is easy once you realize what it really entails, but it is not necessarily intuitive. This is why you must start building recognition into the culture of your organization. It is important that managers and supervisors understand the principles of recognition, but it is equally important that all employees believe that recognition is part of the value system within the company. To evaluate the state of your current recognition culture, ask yourself the following questions:

1. **Do your managers know how and why to recognize their employees?**

   Evaluate both types of managers: those who do not believe in recognition and therefore do not give any, and those who give too much. A manager who does his best to motivate people, but "over-recognizes" by awarding everyone even when they don't deserve it is equally as ineffective at recognition as the manager who does nothing at all.

2. **Do you offer recognition training?**

Recognition training is recommended for both new and experienced supervisors. Recognition is far too important to throw your dollars at the reward programs when your managers don't understand how and don't have the skill to recognize effectively.

3. **Does your Human Resource Department conduct employee recognition surveys?**

Communication and feedback are critical to developing and managing an effective recognition program. Asking employees what they want in their recognition program is one of the most important things the Human Resource Department can do when creating and managing a recognition program. Surveys, focus groups, forums, interviews, etc. are all effective means to solicit recognition feedback. Use the information as the primary source to learn what works well and what part of the program is ineffective so improvements can be implemented. A annual company wide employee recognition survey is recommended. The key is to ask the right questions and create a base line so you can compare progress from one year to the next.

4. **Do you have a communication process for employees to give feedback and share their thoughts and ideas about recognition throughout the year?**

Feedback can be done via suggestions boxes, websites, email, or even a recognition hotline number. The most important aspect of the feedback loop is to make sure that all suggestions are acknowledged and that good suggestions are acted upon. When employees see that their ideas are making a difference, they will share the good news with others, which will increase employee "buy-in."

5. **Do your recognition efforts go beyond those departments where quantitative, measurable results that directly impact the bottom line are obvious?**

Organizations are notorious for creating elaborate reward programs for employees in sales departments. These types of companies place high value on jobs that have a direct link to profits but that sends the message to all other employees that their contributions are subclass. Be sure that your award criteria is inclusive so all employees can fairly participate in the program. You may have to create different reward and recognition criteria for different departments — the bottom line is that you need to make rewards attainable for everyone.

After you have evaluated the current state and determined if your recognition efforts are on target, way out in left field, or perhaps nonexistent, it is now time to make changes. You need to start at the top and make recognition a part of your corporate values. When you redefine your overall purpose to include valuing your employees and recognizing their accomplishments, you send a strong message to everyone within the company that people matter. Start today by recognizing your own employees, and create a recognition buzz that transmits company wide.

The Recognition Train

The leaders and managers within a company will be expected to champion recognition but individual employees are not exempt from the process. When employees begin to feel the difference that recognition makes in their work life, they will naturally try to pass on that feeling when dealing with coworkers of their own. The very act of recognizing someone creates a special feeling within us as well. We know that we are making someone else feel valued and that makes us feel wonderful. The fallout of these warm, fuzzy feelings is very helpful in mitigating the everyday stressors people feel at work and can improve morale, motivation, and productivity in and of itself.

Working in a cold and indifferent environment does nothing to improve burnout or lack of enthusiasm, but working in a warm environment full of camaraderie and positive energy has the power to boost anyone out of a slump. You see, when you begin recognizing and valuing people, the response can only be positive and even the most negative and jaded people have no choice but to be influenced. Deliberate recognition starts the process, and pretty soon, recognition becomes so intuitive that people don't even realize they are "recognizing" someone; they just know they are treating others with respect and appreciation, and that is precisely what this whole motivation discussion is all about. To motivate someone, you must first "get" that person, and when you get others, they get you, and they are more likely to work for and with you to accomplish whatever needs to be done.

Recognition is all about the human factor, and that means recognition can move upwards too! Do not forget to let your manager know that you appreciate him or her and the support he or she provides. Managers at all levels are bombarded with complaints, and all the other unsavory stuff that comes with the job. A little genuine recognition thrown their way will increase the likelihood even more that he or she reciprocates with recognition of his own. Don't give recognition upwards in order to receive something as that is not genuine and will only get you labeled a brown-noser. Do give recognition up with no other intention but to make someone's day. Too often, we take good management for granted when instead it should be shouted from the rooftops and held up for example.

A corporate culture that is strong in recognition is one where all employees flourish. Don't take anyone or anything for granted within your organization. Encourage people on a daily basis and watch them reach and strive for more and more fulfillment. Just as trying to answer the irrelevant question, "How do you motivate employees?" puts you in a vicious cycle of trying one motivation method after another, effective recognition creates a cycle of its own but it is a positive cycle that generates positive energy and yields continually greater positive results.

Right Behavior Turned Wrong

It is easy to inadvertently steer your employees to act in ways that on the surface appear great, but that actually breed inefficiency, complacency, dishonesty, or worse. Here are some examples:

- If you begin informal or formal recognition for meeting budgets, you may encourage shortcuts within departments that are not in the company's best interest.

- Recognizing long-standing service may encourage mediocrity and not necessarily high performance.

- Recognizing low numbers of safety infractions might encourage the suppression of incidents, potentially increasing the chances of a major accident down the road.

- If you recognize sales leads rather than profitability, you end up encouraging quantity over quality and decreasing your competitiveness.

These are just a few examples of how well-meaning recognition, done in very effective ways, can lead to ineffective and inappropriate personal, team, and organization behavior. Before instituting any reward and/ or recognition program, be diligent in defining exactly what you want to reward/recognize and why.

I know I just spent a whole section of this book telling you to recognize spontaneously and not overanalyze the process, but that applies to the way in which recognition is given, not to *what* is actually recognized. Not every organization will want to recognize the same behavior. It is important that you spend sufficient time at the beginning to plan and prepare your recognition program. The best and most efficient method for doing this involves five steps:

1. Define Organizational Values and Goals

A successful reward/recognition program is based primarily on an organization's goals and values. **What is the ultimate reason the organization exists, and what does it hope to accomplish?** You need this information in order to determine what behaviors are most compatible with the organization's strategic goals, because those are the behaviors you want to target for formal and informal recognition.

2. Benchmark Top Performance

In this step, you identify current top performers and define what it is that they do that is exemplary, unique, compelling, etc. **What is it specifically that sets some employees apart from their peers?** These specific behaviors are then used as benchmarks for determining what you want to recognize, promote, and ultimately what you want to motivate others to do.

3. Define Your "Right" Behaviors

Now that you understand what your top performers are doing that is noteworthy, you need to analyze these behaviors and determine whether widespread, similar performance will help achieve organizational goals. It is at this point that you must identify potential negative repercussions of the behavior you are rewarding. **Is the behavior going to encourage short-term gain at the expense of long-term profitability, competitiveness, or sustainability?** Put each behavior through a rigorous test to make sure it is compatible with "why" you are implementing the program in the first place.

4. Communicate Your Expectations

The next required component is to clearly define what you expect from all employees and then tell them. As with any change initiative, you must effectively communicate what you are trying to accomplish and why. With any reward and recognition, it is imperative that you go one step further and outline specifically what you expect from employees. This is no time to test how well your employees understand the organization's goals. You need to be clear and explicit when explaining what types of behaviors you want to promote. **What is it exactly that employees need to be doing on a consistent basis?** Communicate this to them and help them understand their role within the larger context of the organization as a whole.

5. Set Employees Up For Success

The last, and probably most critical, component to consider when beginning to design a reward and recognition program is to catch employees doing things right. Provide lots of opportunity for informal recognition, and make sure even the smallest efforts get recognized. **What are employees doing to head in the right direction?** The reason for reward and recognition is to build intrinsic motivation, and remember: the most motivating thing for people is praise and appreciation. Start with the small changes or the everyday achievements, and gradually build your expectations. You will find your employees' expectations of themselves will increase over time.

Reward and recognition itself is not complex, but it *is* challenging. It challenges how appreciative you are of your employee's and coworker's efforts, it challenges how you interact with them, and it challenges how you define success. However, it is a very worthy and important challenge — one that you should begin tackling today.

Chapter 5

Setting Up a Recognition Program

"Recognition is something a manager should be doing all the time — it's a running dialogue with people."

-Ron Zemke, Senior Editor of Training magazine

Now that you are armed with lots of theory, in-depth understanding and practical solutions for employee recognition, it is time to build a recognition program that meets the needs of your organization. This process is done best with a three-stage approach:

1. **Assess your current recognition efforts.**

2. **Identify and plan your recognition strategy.**

3. **Acknowledge that your recognition plan requires continuous evaluation.**

Assess Your Current Efforts

When you are trying to assess your current recognition practices, you need to go directly to the source. This is not an exercise for you and/or your management team, because you will almost certainly view your level of recognition and appreciation much differently than those on the receiving end. There are a number of reasons for the difference in perception. Common problems related to ill-perceived recognition include the actual delivery of a recognition message, problems with what gets recognized in the workplace, the overall recognition culture, degree of communication, and fairness of the recognition. Any effort you make toward recognizing and outwardly appreciating your employees is to be commended, but you can't give yourself a whole-hearted pat on the back until you know what your employees think and say about your efforts when they talk among themselves or with friends and family.

In order to obtain a complete picture of your recognition efforts, it is also a good idea to assess employee satisfaction with the various factors that coincide with recognition and motivation in the workplace. For instance, you can't support a high recognition culture if you don't communicate well with your employees. A workplace that doesn't encourage diversity or expression of one's opinion is not likely to support and use recognition or motivational practices. A high stress inducing workplace will discourage motivational efforts of which recognition is one of the most important. It is more than just direct recognition activities that count — it is the entire atmosphere, the practices, and the overall workplace culture that need to be examined before embarking on a recognition program designed to improve or enhance positive employee motivation.

The best way to gather this type of information is with a cross-reference survey whereby you and other managers complete a recognition practice inventory and then have your employees fill out the same survey. What this process will reveal are the areas in which you are already doing a good job with recognition and areas where you are falling short. Perhaps what you, your colleagues, and senior management consider appropriate and highly effective are not at all well-received by your employees. Or, maybe you think you are doing a good job of communicating with your employees when their perception is much different. You need to uncover these inconsistencies and develop a plan to remedy them in order to build a strong recognition culture and a highly motivated workplace.

The following is a survey example that you can use or adapt for your own purposes:

Current Recognition Practices and Employee Satisfaction Survey

Answer the survey questions using the following options:

☐ Always   ☐ Seldom

☐ Frequently   ☐ Never

☐ Occasionally

Recognition Activity

1. Employees are given verbal praise.

2. Employees are given written praise (thank-you notes, cards, etc.).

3. Employees are given praise through email.

4. Employees are given praise in public (at meetings, special events, informal groups, etc.).

5. Employees are given certificates for specific accomplishments or achievements.

6. Employees are given small monetary rewards for achievement (gift certificates, coupons, dinner, flowers, etc.).

7. Employees are rewarded with paid time off from work.

8. Employees are offered flexible work schedules.

9. Employees are offered choice of work/assignments where appropriate.

Recognition Effectiveness

10. Employees are given recognition in a genuine manner.

11. Employee recognition is given in a timely manner.

12. Employees appreciate the type of recognition they receive.

13. Attempts are made to individualize the recognition provided.

14. Employees feel more valued after a recognition activity.

15. Employees have equal opportunity to receive recognition within our organization.

Feedback Activity

16. Employees are given useful and constructive feedback.

17. Employees are given adequate feedback about their performance.

18. Employees receive feedback that helps them improve their performance.

19. Employee feedback is given in a timely manner.

20. Employees have an opportunity to participate in the goal setting process.

21. Employee performance evaluations are fair and appropriate.

22. When employees do a good job, they receive the praise and recognition they deserve.

Degree of Teamwork

23. Our organization practices and encourages teamwork.

24. There is a strong feeling of teamwork and cooperation in our organization.

Degree of Customer Focus

25. Letters from customers are circulated or posted for all employees to see.

26. Employees are held accountable for the quality of work they produce.

27. Our organization maintains a very high standard of quality.

28. Our organization understands its customers' needs.

Awareness of Mission and Purpose

29. Employees have a good understanding of the mission and the goals of our organization.

30. Employees understand how their work directly contributes to the overall success of our organization.

31. Employees are provided with regular updates and information about the mission and the goals of our organization.

32. Employees understand the organization's strategic goals.

33. Employees derive personal satisfaction from achieving organization goals.

Compensation

34. Employees are paid fairly for the work they do.

35. Employees' salaries are competitive with similar jobs.

36. Employees' benefits are comparable to those offered by other organizations.

37. Employees understand and use their benefit plan for optimum results.

38. Employees are satisfied with their benefit package.

Workplace Resources

39. Employees are given the resources required to do their job well.

40. The requisite information systems are in place and accessible for employees to accomplish their tasks.

41. The workplace is well maintained.

42. The workplace is a physically comfortable place to work.

43. The workplace is safe.

Opportunities for Growth

44. Employees are given adequate opportunities for professional growth in our organization.

45. Employees receive the training they need to do their job well.

46. Managers are actively involved in the professional development and advancement of their employees.

47. Managers encourage and support employee development.

48. Employees are encouraged to learn from their mistakes.

49. Employees have mentors or coaches at work from whom they can learn.

50. Employees consider their work challenging.

51. Employees consider their work stimulating.

52. Employees consider their work rewarding.

Work/Life Balance

53. The environment in our organization supports a balance between work and personal life.

54. Managers encourage employees to maintain a balance between work and personal life.

55. Employees are able to satisfy both their job and family responsibilities.

56. Employees are provided a work pace that is conducive to good work.

57. Employee workloads are reasonable.

58. Expectations placed on employees are reasonable.

59. Employees do not suffer unreasonable stress due to the functions of their jobs and their position within our organization.

Fairness and Consistency

60. Employees are treated fairly within our organization.

61. Policies are administered as consistently as possible within our organization.

62. Employees are awarded raises, promotions, special assignments, etc. in accordance with stated policies.

63. Favoritism or other workplace relationships are not used as factors when dealing with workplace issues.

Respect for Employees

64. Employees are always treated with respect.

65. Employees are listened to within our organization.

66. The culture of our organization fosters respect for employees.

67. Employee's special skills, abilities, and talents are valued within our organization.

68. Managers and coworkers care about each other as people.

Communication

69. Information and knowledge are shared openly within our organization.

70. Communication is encouraged within our organization.

71. Managers do a good job of sharing information.

72. Senior management communicates well with the rest of the organization.

Personal Expression

73. Employees are allowed to challenge or question current practices or decisions.

74. Employees can disagree with their manager without fear of reprisal.

75. Employees can express their opinions openly at work.

76. Employees in our organization have diverse backgrounds.

As you can see from the questions in the survey, what you are trying to assess is the overall morale and satisfaction within the workplace. By comparing manager's responses to those of the employees, it will become apparent where there are issues of conflict. Make detailed notes of these areas of concern and refer to them constantly as you begin to plan and execute recognition guidelines that will work for you.

You may even want to go one step further with each conflict area and gather more in-depth information about the issues that are most concerning for employees. Any steps you can take to make your workplace more open and communicative are worthwhile.

Identify and Plan Your Strategy

Now that you have a good understanding and awareness of your current recognition practices and overall employee satisfaction, you are ready to formulate a plan for establishing an effective recognition strategy. The information you gathered indicates where you are doing a good job and the areas that need improvement. You can then begin to set out recognition guidelines that will encourage the type of behavior and activity your organization desires and hopefully eliminate negative and detracting behaviors.

Before embarking on this next step, remember to keep in mind the basic rule of motivation: **Different people are motivated by different things at different times.**

The impact of this rule is significant, because it means that your job is not to create a one-size-fits-all recognition program, but rather to set out guidelines for recognition that have enough flexibility and creativity so as to accommodate all the users and recipients. To accomplish this multi-variant task, you will need to be quite organized, and the best way to approach the process is with a structured plan.

Step 1: Form a Committee

When you develop a recognition program, it is beneficial to have a committee or other type of team assist you with the overall program development and management. The program will be for everyone and therefore it is important that there be a broad representation of ideas from within the company. Managers and employees should share jointly in the development and administration of the program to ensure that the interests and preferences of all groups are represented and incorporated appropriately. The committee will determine the general direction of the recognition efforts and will manage the communication and feedback process once the program begins.

This Recognition Program Development Committee will assist with program management and development in the following ways:

- Publicize the program.

- Conduct and administer feedback information solicited during the process.

- Determine overall recognition guidelines including formal and informal recognition efforts.

- Suggest recognition program components as well as various rewards or activities that are inline with the overall values and principles within your organization.

- Provide rewards and make arrangements for special events that pertain to or support employee recognition activity.

Being part of this recognition committee can also be used as a powerful tool in employee recognition and appreciation. Many employees are motivated by increased responsibility or new tasks, and the opportunity to participate on the committee can be an incentive or perk for the right employee. What you want to avoid is any perception of favoritism, so make sure whatever process you use is transparent and gives equal opportunity to all who would express a desire to be a part of the process. Other factors to consider for committee membership include:

- Length of term

- A process for membership

- Who is tasked with overall responsibility for the committee

- How committee membership is actually attained (election, appointment, volunteer, etc.)

Step 2: Conduct an Employee Opinion Survey

I know there have been a lot of surveys suggested for you to perform as you venture along this path to create a high motivation workplace. However, I can't emphasize enough the importance of getting feedback and input from employees — it is the only way you will learn what is most valuable to them, and without individual value, your recognition and motivation efforts will be lackluster at best.

In order for your recognition committee to develop an effective recognition strategy, you must go to the source and find out what types of recognition will meets the needs, expectations and preferences of your employees. The easiest and most efficient way to do this is through a survey. I have created an example below, but please use your imagination, creativity, and hopefully some specific ideas from the second half of this book to construct your own survey.

Employee Recognition Survey

People are individuals, which means everyone has their own unique preference for being recognized. Because everyone's needs are different, we would like you to fill out the following survey to give us an indication of the type of recognition you value and what you would consider a motivator. Additionally, we would like to know what you would like to do to help us create a supportive and appreciative workplace where everyone feels respected and valued. Responses will be shared with your immediate supervisor or manager only.

I prefer to be recognized by (check all that apply):

☐ Public praise

☐ Praise given privately in person

☐ Note of thanks

☐ Letter of commendation to department head

☐ Email message to unit

☐ Personal email

☐ Mention in newsletter or on website

☐ A small, personalized gift (e.g. coffee mug, plaque, certificate)

☐ Food items

☐ Gift certificates

☐ Formal recognition programs and ceremonies (employee of the month/year)

☐ Opportunity to attend training of choice

☐ Opportunity to participate on committees and task forces

☐ Opportunity to work on teams or with others

☐ Have lunch with supervisor

☐ Nomination for specific awards for process improvement, customer service, safety, attendance, cost-saving ideas, etc.

☐ Other:

_____

_____

_____

_____

I would enjoy participating in a recognition program that helps me recognize my co-workers' efforts.

I am willing to serve on a unit committee to develop and maintain recognition in our workplace.

Please list other ways to show general appreciation to all employees and coworkers:

_____

_____

_____

Thank you for your input.

Conducting an employee opinion survey can assist a recognition committee in identifying preferred types of awards, establishing nomination and selection procedures, and determining the frequency and method(s) of award presentation preferred by employees.

Step 3: Identify Your Purpose

Once you have begun laying the groundwork for a recognition program (developed the committee, surveyed employees, and analyzed survey results), you need to create a mission statement for your committee to follow. As you have been discovering throughout this book, motivation and recognition are highly subjective processes that can be misrepresented, misunderstood, and misapplied very easily. Your committee members will need a clear and focused mission to guide them when making decisions.

Some factors to consider when developing your recognition program's mission are:

- Tailor the program to suit the needs of employees and to complement the type(s) of work done in each department.

- Make a clear link between the recognition program's mission and that of the organization and its individual departments.

- Remember that what gets rewarded or recognized gets done. Emphasize core skills and functions by incorporating them into the recognition or reward initiatives.

- The mission must support the goal of any recognition program which is to provide a program that is fair and flexible, that meets the needs of employees, and provides an opportunity to formally recognize and reward their efforts and accomplishments.

- Ensure the mission includes both formal and informal recognition practices.

Step 4: Define Themes and Criteria

Identifying themes and criteria for achievement and formal recognition are necessary so that employees understand why an award has been given. It also helps them to determine what they can do to earn recognition for their own efforts. Make sure you communicate your intentions and the rationale for the criteria — this encourages buy-in and also helps employees understand your mission. Some recognition themes that you may want consider are as follows:

- Overall Excellence
- Attendance
- Customer Service
- Distinguished Service
- Teamwork
- Technical Achievement
- Creativity or Innovation
- Leadership
- Commitment and Dedication
- Above and Beyond a Job Description
- Flexibility or Adaptability to Change

- Employee/Team Player of the Month/ Quarter/Period/Year
- Money-Saving Suggestion Award
- Personal Achievement Award
- Educational Achievement
- Community Service
- Workplace Safety Award
- Morale Booster
- Most Fun
- Professional Development
- Skill Improvement

Step 5: Determine Eligibility Factors

After the recognition theme(s) have been chosen, the recognition committee needs to set in place a process for both informal and formal recognition to take place. Key components to setting up a successful recognition program are fairness, consistency, and an equal chance for reward. This process will take much communication between the committee, senior management, and department managers, and it requires extensive communication with employees. The slightest hint of bias in the recognition eligibility can derail your whole process and make it that much more difficult to introduce modifications. The end result will be more de-motivation than you had in the first place.

Questions to consider when developing eligibility requirements are as follows:

Informal Recognition

- Do the managers and supervisors have the tools required to feel comfortable with informal recognition?
- Do the managers and supervisor's managers model informal recognition practices?
- Do the managers and supervisors understand the intention and purpose of company recognition?
- Are there clear expectations set out for managers and supervisors regarding recognizing employees?

Formal Recognition

- Is there a nomination process?
- Who is eligible to nominate whom?
- Do some rewards have restrictions for eligibility (part-time vs. full-time staff). How is this justified and communicated? What programs are available for those not eligible for some rewards?
- Are committee members eligible for formal recognition?
- How often will a formal reward be presented?
- Who makes the ultimate decision regarding the "winner"?

Step 6: Identify Reward Choices

A critical role of the recognition committee is to provide appropriate suggestions for supervisors and managers to use when implementing either formal or informal recognition practices. It is important that each manager is free to choose recognition that is congruent with his or her values and management style, but there is also a distinct need to keep reward and recognition fairly consistent with the company as a whole.

For instance, the manager in accounting can't be rewarding high performers with trips to Hawaii if all the guys in distribution get are T-shirts and movie passes. It is the job of the recognition committee to work with senior managers, department managers, and employees to figure out what levels of reward and recognition are available and for what. As always, leave room for individual creativity, but set some boundaries for managers and supervisors to follow. Following is a list of reward channels commonly used within companies:

Ceremonies:
Luncheon or Dinner

Retirement Party

Holiday Party

Gifts:
Event Tickets

Gift Certificates

Trophies/Plaques

Monetary and Paid Leave Awards

Publicity:
Newsletters

Other publications

Departmental Annual Report

Display a plaque or trophy publicly

Letter or certificate given personally to an employee by a supervisor or manager

Recognition at staff meeting

Day of Appreciation

Step 7: Monitor and Enhance

Your recognition program needs to be monitored and evaluated on a regular basis to assess its effectiveness and to obtain feedback and suggestions from employees. The Recognition Program Committee is the facilitator of this process, but it needs to be done in conjunction with senior managers and departmental staff. Ideally, there is a feedback system incorporated into the daily operations of the recognition program, but at the very least, an evaluation needs to take place on a yearly basis. This last step brings us to the final stage of setting up your recognition plan: recognizing that you need to have continuous evaluation.

Recognize When Your Program Needs Revamping

Even though you have followed the process to a "T," your recognition program will not remain effective forever. The premise of this book is that motivation changes between people and over time so you must keep your program fresh and relevant. This requires a commitment to continuous review and evaluation. You need to do this analysis both formally and informally. Surveys can be given out periodically, but the best way to gauge the level of stagnancy is to keep your ear to the ground and remain in-tune with your employees. Some common signs that your recognition program is in need of a revamping include the following:

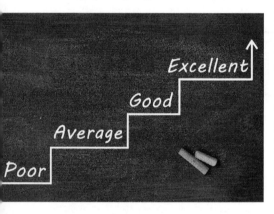

Enthusiasm is lost

Do your employees still talk about the program? Do they seem energized and motivated to earn recognition or reward?

Have old habits started to creep back into the workplace?

If you answered "yes" to any of these questions, then you need to engage your employees and discuss what is going on, figure out what you need to do create excitement again, and then do it.

Participation is dwindling

Are fewer nominations coming in for rewards? Is informal recognition waning? Are managers losing their motivation to participate?

An effective recognition program is supposed to breed excitement and take on a life of its own. When this positive recognition cycle ceases, you know your program needs a boost. Look at ways to encourage recognition throughout the company, and make sure the recognition effort is not just top down.

The program is the butt of jokes and the source of complaints

Do employees run around the hallways mocking your recognition efforts? Is using a company coffee mug a source of hysterics? Do employees create mock certificates for the "Best Butt Kisser" or take coworkers out to lunch to celebrate a missed deadline? Is your suggestion box full of allegations of inequality and favoritism?

When employees start making fun of your recognition efforts, you know it is no longer a source of value. When they start complaining about the mechanics of your program, you are in big trouble. Recognition that is perceived as unfair is a prime source of employee dissatisfaction and will have an extremely negative effect on your workplace motivation efforts. Return to your mission and purpose and look at the actual operation of the program. If you need to go back to stage one, do it — do whatever it takes to keep the program valuable.

Employees expect the perks

Do your employees expect the recognition perks without putting in any special effort?

This is the most insidious and dangerous of all recognition program pitfalls. It is also the hardest to detect. There is a fine line between recognizing employees for a job well done and recognizing employees for doing their job. When you start a recognition program, it is common to want to catch employees doing something right. If, however, you don't replace your over-recognition with recognition that is tied to exceptional behavior (as defined by your recognition criteria), then you run the risk of employees expecting recognition for everything they do. Keep a close eye on this phenomenon and monitor yourself and others to make sure recognition remains appropriate.

Program Reassessment

The beginning stage for any program change is data collection. Solicit feedback from your employees and managers through surveys, group discussion, or one-on-one interviews. Try to find answers to the following questions:

- Which aspects of the program are well received?
- Which elements are ineffective or unpopular?
- Are there any sources of contention with the process?
- Who uses the program?
- If someone is not using the program, why aren't they?
- Are the actual rewards losing value and significance?
- Are the mechanics of the program problematic?

Gather as much information about the current usage and perception of the program as possible. You will use this data to make the necessary changes.

Once you know what the sources of ineffectiveness or dissatisfaction are, you need to make a plan to change them. Many times, an infusion of new life into the program is enough to reenergize employees and managers. Brainstorm new ideas that will encourage the recognition culture in general, and try out innovative rewards and incentives. You may need to get a little wacky just to liven things up — fun is always appreciated, and it certainly brings a renewed sense of energy to even the most mundane of situations.

Regardless of what specific changes or interventions you make, remember that no recognition program will last forever. They all necessarily get dull after a period of time, so expect to change every so often. By planning for change, you won't get disheartened with the recognition effort. Make sure you keep senior management involved in the program, and encourage them to participate openly in the programs' efforts. There is no greater incentive than a senior role model, so make sure you have top management's participation and support.

Chapter 6

Choosing Your Rewards

Management guru Peter Drucker once said, "Economic incentives are becoming rights rather than rewards." The significance of that statement on workplace motivation is that in order to get and keep employees motivated in today's work environment, you need to look beyond what they are paid and focus on recognizing them for their contributions to the organization.

Even after you have created a foundation for a motivation-rich workplace, you can't be complacent. Motivation changes constantly and it is a dynamic process that needs continual tweaking and recharging. There are a wide variety of tools and techniques you can use that enhance the natural motivation inherent in each and every employee, and I hope to provide you with a source of many alternatives from which you can choose and adapt to your employees' specific needs and preferences.

To give you an idea of how significant external rewards are to employee satisfaction, engagement, and motivation, here are the results of an employee survey conducted by the Society of Human Resource Management in 2015.

The 600 U.S. employees who took the survey ranked their answers on a "Very Important" and "Very Satisfied" scale. The average percentages are below.

2015 Employee Job Satisfaction and Engagement

Question	Importance/ Satisfaction
Respectful treatment of all employees at all levels	72% / 33%
Trust between employees and senior management	64% / 28%
Benefits overall	63% / 27%
Compensation/pay overall	61% / 24%
Job security	59% / 32%
Relationship with immediate supervisor	58% / 40%
Opportunities to use your skills and abilities in your work	58% / 34%
Immediate supervisor's respect for my idea	56% / 37%
Organization's financial stability	55% / 33%
Management's recognition of employee job performance	55% / 24%
Communication between employees and senior management	55% / 23%
Feeling safe in your work environment	53% / 48%
Management's communication of organization's goals and strategies	52% / 26%
The work itself	50% / 36%
Overall corporate culture	48% / 31%

Career advancement opportunities within the organization	47% / 20%
Autonomy and independence	47% / 28%
Meaningfulness of job	46% / 35%
Relationships with coworkers	44% / 42%
Teamwork within department/business unit	43% / 26%
Organization's commitment to professional development	42% / 23%
Teamwork between departments/business units	41% / 22%
Job specific training	41% / 22%
Communication between departments/business units	41% / 21%
Career development opportunities	39% / 21%
Contribution of work to organization's business goals	38% / 33%
Variety of work	37% / 32%
Networking opportunities	33% / 21%
Company-paid general training	31% / 24%
Organization's commitment to corporate social responsibility	31% / 26%
Organization's commitment to a diverse and inclusive workforce	29% / 28%
Organization's commitment to a "green" workplace	20% / 19%

Note: n = 600. Importance percentages are based on a scale where 1 = "very unimportant" and 4 = "very important." Satisfaction percentages are based on a scale were 1 = "very dissatisfied" and 5 = "very satisfied." Data are sorted in descending order by the percentage of respondents who indicated "very important." Source: *Employee Job Satisfaction and Engagement* (SHRM, 2015)

Some of the questions the Society of Human Resource Management asked are actions that will be discussed in this part of the book with formal, extrinsic motivation. A few others are intrinsic factors that were discussed in the first half. By combining the power of these two sources of motivation, you will tap directly into the source of positive motivation that will spur your employee's productivity and performance to levels you never imagined.

Having made my point about the power of extrinsic motivation, the following sections provide numerous specific ways for you to begin motivating your employees. Use my suggestions as a starting point, and let your own creativity and knowledge of your employees come through to design reward and recognition practices that are as unique as your company and its people.

Gifts

The most common way to reward employees is through the giving of a gift. People love gifts, and they love to be surprised. What they don't love is to be surprised with a gift that is inappropriate or useless. Before you become the office Santa, look over the following gift ideas and decide what will be most appreciated by specific employees. I've included gifts in many price ranges, and most can be adapted to suit your budget requirements.

1. Gift certificates – this is an old standard, but it definitely ensures the recipient gets what he or she wants.

2. Chocolates – you can give a simple candy bar or you can create an elaborate basket of chocolates from a gourmet chocolatier.

3. Lottery tickets – have scratch and win tickets on hand to give out as spontaneous recognition. Consider creating a lottery fund and having all employees participate. For special recognition, purchase tickets to the larger home lotteries that are sponsored by charitable organizations.

Not only do you recognize your employees but you also contribute to worthwhile causes.

4. Dinner for two – who doesn't appreciate a dinner for two certificate? Make sure you choose the type of restaurant that would most suit the person receiving the reward. Some people enjoy pretentious silver service with waiters who use special crumb scrapers between courses and others prefer the more relaxed atmosphere of popular national chain restaurants.

5. Massage certificate – you can get a variety of massage packages from a simple foot massage to an all-over body massage or massages with herbal and aromatherapy elements. Go as fancy or plain as you think is appropriate.

6. Meals sent to your home – for busy families, this type of recognition is a God-send. Popular companies include HelloFresh™ and Blue Apron. Both offer a wide range of meal choices that are all balanced and nutritious. You can reward your employee with a gift certificate so that they can order their first box of food for free.

7. Catered dinner – have a chef come to your employee's home and prepare a gourmet meal especially for his or her family. What a treat. If you want to make it extra special, provide a catered dinner for eight so your employee can invite some friends to join in on the celebration.

8. Cookies delivered to employee's door – many online companies offer gourmet cookie service. You can get a weekly order or monthly order and you can even try the special cookie of the month. A fun way to receive a reward that continues over time.

9. Balloon bouquet – have it delivered to the office or home. If you want to make this type of recognition silly, fill the employee's office with balloons and have colleagues watch as he or she makes his way to the desk.

10. A year's supply of apparel (employee's choice) – No one likes to spend money on staple items like socks, pantyhose, undershirts, etc. Have the employee choose a staple clothing item as his or her reward.

11. Certificate for tailoring – good for men and women, this will give them a lift as their clothes fit better and they feel better.

12. Shoe shine services for a year – you can get certificates, or you can arrange for the shoe shiner to come to your office once a week for a period of time to shine the shoes of all employees who have earned the recognition.

13. Beauty salon services – try to find out if the employee has a particular establishment she prefers and then surprise her with a certificate for a cut, color, highlight, makeover, etc.

14. Manicure/pedicure gift certificate – most women enjoy getting pampered. A mani/pedi certificate is another God-send for women. Some men enjoy pedicures also (minus the nail polish), so this could be a gift for either men or women.

15. Allow a deserving employee to choose a guest speaker for your next event – the entire organization benefits from the speakers' words, and the employee is rewarded by learning about a topic that is of particular interest to him or her. As an added touch, have the employee introduce the speaker or include him in the presentation in some other way.

16. Barber certificates – again, determine if your employee is a regular somewhere and then prepay the barber so the next time your employee goes to get his hair cut, he will be surprised with a freebie.

17. Spa services – pamper your employees who deserve it. Spas offer so many fabulous services that there should be no difficulty finding something that is just right for the person you want to recognize.

18. Gift on the date of employee's anniversary – this type of recognition goes beyond just giving a reward and shows that you take a personal interest in the employee. Anniversary dates are special, and there is no better way to celebrate than with some token of appreciation. If your budget does not allow for a gift, a hand written card is just as meaningful and will be valued no matter what.

19. Gym membership – depending on budgets and circumstances, you may want to pay for a full year membership, six months, one month, or just the initiation fee. You decide, but make sure the employee will appreciate the gesture before committing him or her to an exercise regime.

20. Workout clothes certificate – for the athletic types in your office, this is an excellent gift. Consider getting a certificate to a high-end store where the person might not shop on a regular basis.

21. Exercise machine – this gift is certainly a high-end item, but it will be a long-term source of remembrance for the employee who receives it. Every morning or evening, when the exercise begins, the recognition principle will be reinforced. Just make sure you are not forcing exercise on an employee, and find out what kind of equipment he or she prefers before making such a large purchase.

22. A number of shares of stock – not only does this type of reward have real cash value; it is also a way to directly link employee performance to company performance. If you choose to award stock, make sure you chart your stock

progress for employees as well. Post the information in a visible location so that employees can see the dollar value of their reward; this can be an effective motivator for improving stock price through improved individual performance.

23. Stamps – this sounds kind of boring at first, but you can get stamps in an array of designs, and they are an everyday staple that most people hate having to pay for themselves. This type of reward is especially valuable at the beginning of December when many employees are sending out Christmas greetings.

24. Computer software for a home computer – depending on your relationship with the corporate software dealer, you may be able to get a good deal on home use software for your employees. Great ideas for software rewards are spyware and antivirus protection, home networking software, accounting packages, design suites, and tax preparation software. Before purchasing in volume, make sure that enough employees will use and appreciate this type of gift.

25. Donation in employee's name to charity of his choice – this is a double feel-good kind of reward. The employee is recognized for his effort, and a charity benefits from the recognition as well. Try to find out beforehand which charities the employee currently supports; this personal touch will make the reward that much more meaningful.

26. Tickets to a gala – many times, special events come to town that are invite only. If your company is on the reserved list, purchase tickets for a special employee and have him and his spouse attend as your guests. This will be perceived as quite an honor, and the employee gets the added bonus of relaxed, out of the office time with senior people from the organization.

27. Box seats for a baseball, football, basketball, or hockey game – if you have an employee who is a sports fan, treat him to a game in the company box seats. While this perk

is usually reserved for customers, there is nothing wrong with sharing it with employees as well.

28. Certificate for cleaning services – with the type of work hours many employees are putting in, a little help around the house is an excellent and unique reward. This also gives the spouse a break and frees up time for family on a weekend.

29. Certificate for landscaping services – a free lawn mowing, spring thatch, or fall mulch is a surprise treat for most people. Everyone likes a well-tended lawn, but make sure the employee has a house with a yard before you offer this kind of reward. If the employee lives in a condo or apartment building, you'll end up looking very foolish, and your recognition effort will be ruined.

30. Certificate for professional home or office organization services – this is a popular personal service that is cropping up everywhere. A professional organizer will come in and help your employee organize a closet, garage, spare room, or office.

31. Certificate for cat or dog food for a year – a great idea, but make sure the employee has a pet. If you are trying to be equitable with the type of reward, opt for a certificate, because feeding a St. Bernard for a year is significantly more expensive than feeding a Chihuahua.

32. One-month payment of mortgage or rent – what a tremendous surprise for an employee who has done something really special. Again, it's a high-ticket item but one that is sure to make a strong and lasting impression.

33. Certificate for a portrait – this is an item that most people don't think to purchase on their own but one that is highly likely to be appreciated by a wide variety of people. You can choose to pay for an entire portrait package or just the sitting fee depending on the budget you are working with. Nowadays, having a professional headshot is a staple in business, particularly with online platforms such as

LinkedIn demanding a small profile photo. The professional headshot can also be used for business cards.

34. Income tax preparation – this is a perfect stress relieving reward. No one enjoys preparing their taxes, and a professional service should find deductions that the average person misses.

35. Personalized license plates for a year – get input from the employee before committing him to a year with "#1 MPLOYE" or "YUR GR8" on the back of his car. Some people like attention and others abhor it; some think personalized anything is tacky and others are proud. As the name suggests, personalized plates are very personal, so it's safest not to surprise anyone with this type of reward.

36. Hot air balloon ride – this is not for the squeamish, but is a thrill for many employees. This is an out of the ordinary gift that most people would not think to purchase for themselves.

37. Paid session with a financial planner – here is another opportunity for a double whammy reward. The employee enjoys a free service that has the potential to change his financial life.

38. A year's subscription to a magazine of employee's choice – everyone likes magazines, but you have to make sure to fit the right magazine to the right person.

39. A one-year membership to a book of the month club – if your employee is an avid reader, this is an excellent reward.

40. Download "X" amount of e-books – a lot of people enjoy reading on their tablet and/or Kindle. Giving them an amount to purchase their e-books could be a great surprise.

41. A one-year subscription to Spotify or Vnyl – for the music lovers out there, these make for a great gift. Spotify will cater to your employees that are more technologically in-tune with the times, while your old-timers might be more

inclined to enjoy the Vnyl subscription, which delivers records to your home each month.

42. A one-year subscription to Audible – many people enjoy listening to books instead of reading them. If you have employees that commute to work and love to learn, this could be your perfect reward.

43. Airline tickets – another high-end item but one that is very appreciated. Make sure the tickets have flexible fly times to accommodate your employee's schedule.

44. Certificate for limousine service – your employees can use this reward to treat themselves to a night on the town or simply take the kids one day and drive around town waving their heads and arms out the sunroof. It's fun, it's unique, and it's versatile; an excellent choice for almost any employee.

45. iPad cover or iPhone case – if your employee owns one of these, odds are they will need a new case at some point. Just make sure you know what brand and what generation their device is before you make the purchase.

46. Cooking lessons – this is an excellent idea, but you don't want to insult anyone. Don't give away cooking lessons to the person on your staff who fancies him or herself a galloping gourmet unless they have expressed an interest in improving their skills. Don't limit this reward to women – it will only showcase your outdated ideas that women are the ones who do most of the cooking. A safe bet for everyone is to award BBQ lessons or a lesson in cooking exotic dishes; something that you would assume most people are not experts at.

47. Pet grooming for a year – make sure the employee has a pet. You don't want the person to feel obligated to use the certificate and come into work on Monday with his hair coiffed like a toy poodle ready for the Westminster Kennel Club Dog Show.

48. Complete automobile detailing service – ahhh, to get back that brand-new car smell. With a complete automobile detail, you can help your employee do just that. A great gift for any employee who owns a car. For those who ride the bus or subway to work because they don't have a car, it just shows how disinterested in them you are, and you will look foolish.

49. Car washes for a year – here again, a great idea; just make sure your employee has a car. Another factor to consider is what type of car wash the employee prefers. Some people will not take their "baby" through an automatic car wash, even the kind that don't touch the car, so a bucket full of quarters for the coin wash will be much more appreciated.

50. Birthday card, cake, gift – remembering an employee's birthday is a very personal gesture that makes the person feel special. You can choose to go all out and have a birthday celebration, or you can simply say "Happy Birthday." Whatever degree of celebration you choose, just make sure you do something. Mark all of your employee's birthdays on your calendar, and set up email notifications if you're likely to forget. Do whatever it takes to make sure you know when an employee is having a birthday.

51. Pay for an employee to attend a conference of his or her choice – this is an excellent form of reward that benefits your company as well. The employee gets training he or she is interested in and the information that is learned at the conference can be shared with other employees. A good practice that you should be implementing whenever someone goes on training is to have that person make a 15 to 20 minute presentation about what he or she learned. This extra bonus of responsibility ensures that your employees don't treat training courses as paid vacation days, and everyone benefits from one person's experiences.

52. Case of beer/bottle of wine – this is usually an appreciated gift, but check your facts first to make sure there is no history of alcohol abuse or that the person is not a recovering alcoholic.

53. Morning coffee for a year – here again, observe your employee's habits. Do they actually drink coffee? Many people opt for tea or soda instead. If it is coffee, most corporate coffee stores have an app that their customers use to pay with and rack up reward points. Loading more money into their account would be an ideal gift.

54. Case of soda or bottled water – good, safe gift ideas that are sure to be used by almost everyone.

55. Weekend hotel stay – this is an excellent way to encourage an employee to take a break and relax. If the employee has kids, you may want to book a stay at a hotel that has a fancy pool and waterslides. Try to set up the reward so the dates are flexible and so that your employee can modify arrangements to suit his needs the best.

56. Gas coupons – great for people who drive gas cars, but not so good for those with diesel, propane, or electric cars. Make sure you know what your employees need before handing out rewards you assume are useful. If you have employees who commute to work, consider purchasing them a public transit pass instead.

57. Oil changes for a year – for car owners, this type of service is great.

58. Tattoo of employee's choice (don't ask where!) – not appropriate in all work settings, but depending on your demographics and line of work, this may be a really cool gift. If you really want to go all out, include piercings.

59. A year's membership to a video streaming service – with all the streaming services available today, this is a great gift to anyone who enjoys binge watching television shows

or the occasional movie night. Popular options include Netflix™, Hulu™, or Amazon Instant Video™.

60. App store gift cards – another great, on the spot recognition gift.

61. Dry cleaning certificates – like dishes and laundry, dry cleaning is a necessary evil in many people's lives. While this is probably a gift alternative that is better received in an office setting rather than manufacturing or construction, don't assume it won't be appreciated. People do wear clothes for purposes other than work, and there are many items around the home, like comforters, that need regular dry cleaning as well.

62. Round of golf – remember, just because you are an avid golfer does not mean all your employees are as well. Golf fanatics tend to think everyone is enamored with the sport but it is wise to make sure the person actually golfs (reasonably well) before you send him out to an exclusive golf club.

63. Ski pass(es) – great idea for winter months where skiing is accessible.

64. Weekend car rental – many people love to get out and drive on the weekend, so rather than putting the miles on their own car, it is a great idea to rent a car and depreciate the value of someone else's vehicle. Another option is to rent an employee a sports car or luxury sedan; something they don't drive on a regular basis.

65. Concierge service – this is a unique option for those employees who seem to have everything already. Employees can have the concierge plan parties, get concert or theatre tickets, and make dinner reservations that they might not be able to secure on their own. A very classy touch.

66. Personal trainer – if you have an employee who is into fitness or perhaps starting a fitness program, this is a

wonderful choice. Anyone who is into diet and exercise will love the attention and advice from an expert. If the person already belongs to a gym, be sure to arrange the trainer through that facility.

67. Massage therapist – there are many options here: gift certificates for massage therapy, regularly scheduled visits where a massage therapist comes to your office, or a surprise visit from a massage therapist right at the office. If you opt for an in-office option, make sure you have a private room available – not many people would want to get (or witness) a full body massage in the reception area.

68. Have soda, fruit, snacks, etc. on hand for employees at all times – many companies have these items stocked for customers and guests; make them available to employees as well.

69. To mark special anniversaries of service, set up committees of coworkers who work within a certain budget, and come up with a dream gift package – this process motivates and recognized the employee who is being honored and the employees who are part of the committee are exhilarated by the event as well.

70. Phone or tablet upgrade – new versions of iPhones, Androids, and tablets are released about every year. This would be another high-end gift for an employee, but it's one they will most definitely appreciate.

71. A year's subscription to a beauty box – obviously a good option for women, but be sure that you only gift this if the woman seems to be particularly interested in beauty and the like. Popular options include Birchbox™ and Ipsy™.

Having trouble deciding what gift to give to whom? There are so many different options for gift giving available, and it should be clear that not all gifts are equally appropriate for all people. The best way to figure out what your employees will most appreciate is to ask them what they like by using a recognition preference profile.

I've put together a very generic profile that you can use or modify for your own organization:

Recognition Preference Profile

From time to time, I would like to recognize your efforts for an outstanding job, and I really want to make the reward valuable and personal. To help me figure out what it is you might like, I need to know:

What is _____favorite…

Restaurant/food:

Fast food breakfast and lunch (Big Mac, fries, etc.) _____

Sit down (Red Lobster, etc.) _____

Pizza/brands, toppings _____

Ethnic foods _____

Desserts/Ice cream treats _____

Bagels, donuts, muffins _____

Snack Foods _____

Coffee Brand (Coffee Beanery, Starbucks, etc.) and drink (Cappuccino, etc.)_____

Soda or beverages _____

Favorite kind of music _____

Miscellaneous Favorites:

Sports teams _____

Flowers _____

Subscription service _____

Magazines_____

Family activity _____

Malls/Dept. stores _____

Video Stores _____

Bookstores _____

Charity or Organization _____

Do you have a nickname? _____

Personal Service:

Do you belong to a gym? Which one? _____

Where do you go and what services do you like (manicure, haircut,

etc.)?_____

When you think of being pampered, what do you imagine?

_____

Tell us a little about yourself: (i.e., your family, children, etc.)

_____

_____

_____

_____

_____

Do you

Collect anything?_____

Play sports? _____

Have a hobby? _____

Enjoy being praised: In private_____ Openly _____
A bit of both _____ Bring it on_____

Like to be surprised? Yes _____ No_____ You won't be able to surprise me! _____

Which of the following types of celebrations do you prefer?

Breakfasts_____

Lunches_____

Dinners_____

Potluck_____

Personal Gift _____

Something else _____

What is your idea of an excellent reward? _____
_____
_____

Have I missed anything? _____
_____
_____
_____

Thanks so much; I look forward to surprising you!

Company Merchandise

Company merchandise is still one the most prevalent forms of employee recognition. There are vast numbers of companies who specialize in supplying gift items with a company logo on them. You do need to be aware that not all employees like these items. Depending on the history of how and intention of why these items were handed out, some workplaces consider them nothing more than a big joke.

Still, company logos do mean something to a great many employees, especially those who work for companies that are respected and that have healthy, fun, and respectful work cultures.

Put your logo on any or all of the following, which make for great gifts:

- Coffee mugs
- Mouse pads
- Pens
- Pencils
- Stress balls
- T-shirts
- Sweatshirts
- Golf shirts
- Rings
- Pins
- Rulers
- Sticky notes
- Golf ball
- Golf tees
- Towels
- Candy
- Lighters
- Note cubes
- Coasters
- Umbrellas
- Luggage
- Coolers
- Frisbees
- Footballs
- Tote bag
- iPhone case
- iPad cover
- Jackets
- Hats
- Fridge magnets

Time Off

Who doesn't enjoy time off from work? You don't have to give full days off to reap the benefit of being considered a fantastic boss. Sometimes, an extra 10 minutes tacked onto a break is all an employee needs to feel rejuvenated and ready to go again. Time off from work does not always mean spending a day idle. Many employees enjoy the ability to work from their home or even take work outside. Just getting out of the office setting is considered a reward under the right circumstances.

Here are some ways you can give time off:

1. Host a "clean out your workspace" day – employees devote their day to cleaning their offices or workstations. Employees are still "working," but they are just doing something that is often neglected because of other pressures and responsibilities.

2. Allow an employee to reorganize their office or workstation – you know how every once in a while you need to rearrange your living room furniture? Well, the same applies to your office space. Placing a desk in a different position and looking at a different wall all day may be enough to light a fire in the most burnt out employee.

3. Hand out a "get out of work free" pass – use your discretion about the time increments on the passes. Hand out 15 minute passes as impromptu awards and save one hour, half day, and full day passes for extra special efforts.

4. Grant a work from home day – if the employee's job is conducive to working at home, let him or her have a break. You may or may not get the same level of output, but your employee will make up the difference upon his or her return.

5. Hand out flex passes – these are passes that employees can redeem for the ability to set their own hours for a day or week or other period you allow. Flexible schedules are a commonly listed perk that employees enjoy and appreciate. If it really doesn't matter if they are at their desk at 8:00 a.m., let them sleep late for a few days and work later into the evening. The important issue is that the work gets done and not necessarily when it gets done. For employees that have a more controlled schedule — i.e. receptionists who must be available to answer the phone — arrange for coverage or cover the phone yourself on a day when he or she chooses to come in late.

6. Give an employee a surprise day off – no pre-warning, nothing: simply tell an employee who has done an excellent job or put in outstanding work that he or she need not come into work the next day. How exhilarating for the employee and fun for you – everyone likes to get and give good surprises.

7. Award three-day weekends – when a day off is given on a Monday or Friday (or other day depending on the employee's schedule), the reward just seems that much better. Three days of rest is more than just 50 percent better, it's at least 100 times better.

8. Allow an employee to leave early that day or come in late the next – you probably won't have to set any specific time. Employees who feel appreciated won't take advantage of the situation, and you build trust by not being a clock-watcher.

9. When you assign an employee a project, make the deadline clear and then allow the employee to finish the assignment in his own way. If the project is completed before the deadline, the employee has the option of taking the rest of the time off.

10. After so many years of service, offer a sabbatical leave for an employee to explore an area of interest.

11. Allow employees to bank sick days and extend their vacation time.

12. Set up a "Donated Vacation Time" bank where employees can donate unused hours for others to use when they find themselves in trying personal circumstances without enough holiday time to cover their leave.

Family Acknowledgment

Employees are not the only ones affected by work life stresses and pressures. The families of the employees often need a break as well. Demonstrating your consideration for the families of your employees goes a long way toward fostering a great work environment. The message is clear: you value your employee as a person, a person who has commitments and responsibilities beyond work, and you understand how difficult balancing those commitments can be.

Here are some ideas to make sure everyone is relaxed and rewarded:

1. Present a gift to your employee's spouse after a bout of overtime.

2. Send tickets for your employee's family to attend a fun event, movie, play, amusement park, attraction, etc.

3. Send a note thanking your employee's spouse for his/her support during overtime.

4. Pay for tutoring hours for children.

5. Provide a certificate toward day care for young children.

6. Provide a certificate for elder care – many employees are tasked with the responsibility of taking care of older parents. This can be quite a burden, and this type of gesture is very personal and meaningful.

7. Pay for a family swim or skate pass for a month.

8. Host a family orientation for new employees with a slide show or video program, and include refreshments; including the whole family in orientation presents your workplace as "family oriented." It says you welcome family members and are in-tune with the personal as well as the professional needs of your employees.

9. Collect drawings from employee's children or grandchildren depicting "What my Mom/Dad/Grandma/

Grandpa/Aunt/Uncle does at work all day." Compile these into a company booklet or display them for customers to enjoy.

10. Tell staff that if they achieve "such a goal," you will call their mothers/spouse/children and tell them how great their child/husband/wife/significant other/mother/father is. Remember how proud you were of doing well on a school assignment and having your teacher tell your parents? Well, this type of recognition taps into those same feels of pride and accomplishment, and the family members will get a kick out of it too!

11. Plan a "bring your family to work" day for your organization. Be sure to include different activities for different age groups. Use activities from your new hire orientation, tours, and even special treats in the cafeteria to help make families feel a part of the organization.

12. Give a bonus, gift, celebration, or some other form of recognition on the birth or adoption of a child. This is an important event in a person's life. Encourage the whole department to share in the good news. Decorate the employee's office or workspace with pink or blue and celebrate his return to work. If your employee is the new mother of a child, invite her to come into the office and show off the baby. Even though she is probably on maternity leave, she is still very much a part of the company, and this gesture shows you care about her and not just her ability to contribute to the organization on a daily basis.

13. Give a reward to employee's children who achieve all "As" on their report card.

14. Plan fun summer family events – instead of just having a picnic or doing the normal stuff, try to come up with a twist, and be sure to include activities appropriate for all ages.

15. Host a children's holiday party – have a meet Santa afternoon full of games, activities, and even a gift exchange. For Easter, host an Easter egg hunt on the grounds or at a local park.

16. Provide a "nursing room" for female employees returning to work but who want to continue nursing their babies and need time and privacy to pump breast milk.

17. Provide expectant dads with a cell phone or beeper so they can be summoned at a moment's notice.

18. Give paid time off for bereavement leave.

Employee Honors

Don't just rely on the "Employee of the Month" standby: award certificates to employees for a variety of office tasks, functions, and expertise. When an employee earns a special recognition, give him or her a special nametag as well as a certificate that pronounces their accomplishment to everyone. Be as fun and creative as you want, but just make sure the award you present will not embarrass the recipient or make him uncomfortable.

1. Service Quality Award – for those employees who consistently complete client work in a timely fashion with very high quality and who make the effort to produce excellence.

2. Practice Development Awards – for those employees who have put forward the most consistent effort in working together as a team to help build the practice.

3. Streamliner Awards – for those employees who came up with the best suggestions for improving the efficiency and effectiveness of the group.

4. Administrative Support Awards – for those employees who provide the most helpful support to others.

5.   Golden Rule Awards – for those employees who always treat others kindly and fairly, who recognize their responsibility to be part of the team, and who know that by helping others succeed, the whole group benefits.

6.   Best Suggestion to Clients Awards – for those employees who saved a client money, increased profitability, found errors which could have resulted in embarrassment or penalties, reduced paperwork, or increased a client employee's productivity.

7.   Mentors of the Year Award – for those employees who caused others to perform at their best, helped them develop to their true potential, or provided a supportive environment that allowed them to take risks and accept challenges.

8.   Sustained Superior Performance Award – award to recognize employees who have consistently exhibited superior performance throughout the course of the year.

9.   Superior Achievement Award – for those employees who perform substantially beyond expectations on a specific assignment or job function, or for a single one-time special act, service, or achievement.

10.   New Horizons Award – for those employees who provide ideas/suggestions that enhance member service, improve employee satisfaction, improve operational processes, and/or reduce costs.

11.   President's Award for Service Excellence – for those employees who have consistently contributed above and beyond what is normally expected in the area of service to members and/or employees during the previous calendar year.

12.   President's Award for Leadership Excellence – for those employees who have exceptional leadership within the organization and who foster an environment of service and managerial excellence.

13. Service Anniversary Award – for those employees who have a certain number of years of tenure with the company (5, 10, 25, etc.)

14. Best Coverage for Colleague on Holiday Award – for those employees who provide seamless coverage while working shorthanded or in a position not regularly held.

15. Best Cross Training (not cross dressing) Effort – for those employees who learned a new skill and apply their talents to help the company.

16. Exemplary Smile – for those employees who just bring joy to the workplace with their smile and friendliness.

17. Corporate Morale Booster – for those employees who always know what to say and do when a colleague needs a pick-me-up

18. Best Computer Glitch Fixer – for those employees who everyone turns to when something goes wrong with the computer.

19. Mr./Ms. Fix-It – for those employees who un-stick drawers, put nails in the wall to hang new certificates, build modular office furniture, un-jam the stapler, etc.

20. Photocopier King or Queen – for those employees who know where the extra paper is, where the toner is, how to put in new toner, and how to reduce, enlarge, collate, copy double-sided, and staple automatically.

21. Fax Machine King or Queen – for those employees who know how where the fax template is, how to send one fax to multiple recipients, how to retrieve stored faxes, and how to send an international fax.

22. Neatest Desk – for those employees for go home every night with all their paperwork filed away and only a blotter on their desk – who are these people anyway? And, where did they come from?

23. Most Organized – for those employees who can produce a document dated four years ago within five minutes of your request. Again, who are these people, and where did they come from?

24. Messiest Workplace – for those employees whose desks look like a bomb recently exploded. In addition to the certificate, you may want to consider getting a professional organizer to help them sort out their lives.

25. Official "Go-to Gal" or "Go-to Guy" – for those employees who everyone "goes to" when no one else seems to have an answer.

26. Best "Out of Office" Message on Voice Mail – for those employees who manage to sound professional on voice mail (i.e: they don't sound like a drone, they don't sound too bubbly, and they don't sound like they are on a caffeine high).

27. Most Innovative E-mail Salutation – for those employees who include more than their official contact information at the end of each email and who also avoid trite motivational or philosophical sayings which recipients are supposed to appreciate and ponder.

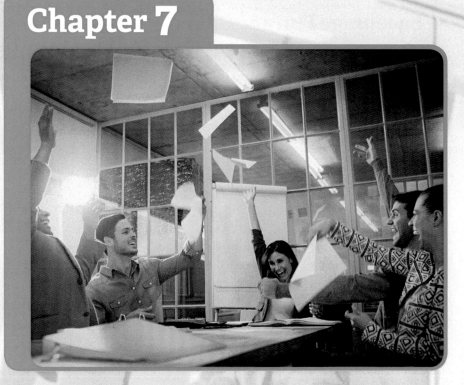

Chapter 7

Having Fun at Work

People need to have fun at work. Work is work, but it doesn't have to be dull and pedantic. The best places to work are those where people don't take themselves too seriously, they allow themselves to be goofy, and they enjoy at least one laugh a day. Fun and humor are known to be strong healers, and they help people get through the toughest times. It is no wonder that infusing some enjoyment and downright fun into a workplace will liven things up and naturally decrease tension and stress. The upside of laughter and amusement is that they encourage creativity and flexibility, which are all central tenants of a productive and highly motivating work culture.

Encourage Fun and Silliness

Here are some ways you can encourage your employees to have fun and laugh a little. Keep in mind that a lot of these suggestions require you to have a sense of humor.

1. Have "no negativity allowed" days — negative comments cost "x" amount of cents or dollars. Funds are placed in jar and used for a fun activity to be enjoyed later that everyone can participate in.

2. Take candid pictures throughout the day. Post the pictures on a bulletin board or as a collage on your social media page for all to enjoy. Don't deliberately embarrass anyone who you know won't appreciate it (again, you need to know your employees), but there are always one or two people at work who will make this activity worthwhile for everyone!

3. Fine those who arrive late to a meeting and distribute the money to those who were there on time.

4. Form a recreation committee to plan monthly activities.

5. Host a company poster party for employees to create signs and posters that demonstrate the company's values. Display them throughout your office or building and move them frequently. Encourage as much creativity as possible. You may want to reward the prizes for the "Best Poster," "Most Ethereal," "Most Artistically Challenged," "Most Creative Use of Color," "Most Frightful."

6. Create a company or department mascot that goes along with the spirit of the company or department. Kidnap other department mascots and send ransom notes.

7. At your next company meeting, plan to "roast" an employee or two.

8. Create a poem about a certain employee's accomplishments. Read it to him and post it on a bulletin board. Frame an original copy for the employee to display.

9. Have a "Laugh a Day" bulletin board where you display appropriate cartoons and humorous writings.

10. Designate one room as the company "Whine Cellar," the place for anyone to go who is having a bad day or wants to gripe. When someone is crabby, suggest they spend some time there.

11. Let employees take 10 to 15 minute "fun breaks" to blow off steam or unwind.

12. Host international days – employees bring in ethnic dishes and learn about the origins and history of the culture.

13. Host an Ugliest Tie contest or Most Worn Shoes contest. Give out certificates and a small prize.

14. Have a "Show and Tell" day at work. Encourage employees to bring in their prized possessions, and explain the significance. Get them to give a bit of history about the item. You can vote on the most unique or have a "Guess who it belongs to" contest before the actual presentations.

15. Sponsor a Tackiest Accessory contest. The winner of these contests receives a small gift.

16. Host a joke day where everyone brings in their favorite joke or cartoon and shares it with colleagues. Collect the jokes and create a joke book that employees can refer to when they need a laugh.

17. Post yearbook photos on a bulletin. Hold a poll to see who has changed the most and who has changed the least. Create captions to go with the photo such as Girl most likely to… and Guy most likely to…

18. Post baby photos. Hold a contest to see who can identify the most employees correctly.

19. Have a talent show at work. You'll be surprised by who plays the accordion, who tap dances, and who can chug a pitcher of beer in thirty seconds flat. Circulate a program and have employees match participants to talents.

20. Bring in a clown or magician to entertain everyone at lunchtime.

21. Have rock/paper/scissors contests.

22. Fly paper airplanes whenever the mood strikes.

23. Name a hallway after an employee who has done a great job.

24. Have dartboard contests. Make up rules and present small prizes.

25. Create special days once a month – have an activity that goes along with the theme.

26. Host a juggling day. Bring in a juggler to teach everyone the art of juggling. Hold a contest at the end for the "Best New Juggler," "Juggler With the Most Unique Technique," and "Least Likely to Be a Professional Juggler."

27. Designate a dress purple day (or whatever color suits your fancy) – vote on who did the best job.

28. Have a bubble gum day – see who can blow the biggest bubble.

29. Have an ice cream treat day – go to the nearest store en-mass at lunchtime and all buy an ice cream treat.

30. Have a picnic day – tell employees to bring a bag lunch and go eat outside on the lawn or go to a park. Supply blankets, sunscreen, and insect repellent if necessary.

31. Have a crazy hat day – vote on the best hat or swap hats every half hour.

32. Host a polka dot day – see how many ways you can incorporate polka dots into your work without it being inappropriate.

33. At employee meetings, tape certificates under chairs at random. Whoever sits in one the special chairs can claim their prize.

34. Have a "What I want to be when I grow up day."

35. Have employees come up with suggestions for special day themes.

36. Host a bake sale – the proceeds can go to charity or for a fun workplace activity.

37. Give your employees Silly String and let them shoot it at people who deserve it.

38. Regularly include jokes or cartoons with memos and emails that you send out.

39. At your next meeting, hand out crazy hats that everyone must wear.

40. Provide staff with kazoos and have them come up with an original tune. Give a prize to the best score.

41. Periodically hold contests like a TV game show where employees answer questions about your operations. This can be an individual or team event.

42. Use an 800# service where employees call in periodically to be given randomly selected test questions. Correct answers make them eligible for a prize. Those who get all questions right receive a reward.

43. Create stickers of appreciation – stick them on employees when they have done a good job. Be as creative and wacky as you want, and have fun with the message.

44. Have a contest with employees – "If my company/ department were a T-shirt, this is what it would say..." Then have them actually design the shirt, either on a real T-shirt or on paper.

45. Host a company Olympics – employees compete in activities around the office and in production to see who can complete the "event" the fastest. Events may include photocopier races, getting coffee for the boss, locating a misplaced file, unloading a pallet of product, packaging a product, etc. Offer small rewards and prizes to the winners.

Holiday Activities

The holidays are always a great time take some time off and have a little fun in the office. Office parties, cookouts, and gift exchanges are all events your employees would enjoy doing together. Taking the time to organize an event with a holiday around the corner can also make your employees feel more relaxed during this time. People

are often stressed during the holiday season because of travel, family, finances, and gifts on top of their everyday responsibilities. A fun holiday treat may be just what they need.

However, make sure you're aware of all of your employees' religious beliefs before you plan the activity. If you have a few employees who celebrate different holiday traditions than the majority, make sure their beliefs are incorporated into your celebration so they don't feel excluded.

Holiday recognition ideas

1. Have an Easter egg hunt for employees – let them find candy as well as other small recognition items or coupons they can redeem for work favors later.

2. Bring rabbits, chicks, and other baby animals into the office for a day. Invite employee's children to visit.

3. Dress like a pilgrim for Thanksgiving.

4. Bring a turkey dish for a potluck lunch the day before the long weekend.

5. Have a "Decorate the office day" to prepare for Christmas.

6. Hold a gift exchange day sometime before Christmas.

7. Have a costume contest for Halloween.

8. Host a pumpkin-carving contest – provide a small prize to the best pumpkin.

9. Dress in red for Valentine's Day.

10. Wear stars, stripes, red, white, or blue for the 4th of July.

11. Have green-colored popcorn or ice cream on St. Patrick's Day.

12. Celebrate non-Christian holidays with employees from different ethnicities and cultures.

13. Ask minority employees to host awareness sessions for their specific observances, and make time for all employees to attend.

Bizarre and Largely Unknown "Days"

There are many official "days" that most of us have never heard of, but they are actual, sponsored days of observance. Use these "days" to develop unique and fun activities for your employees to participate in. On special days or within designated months, use rewards that coincide with the item or activity being honored. For instance, January is Gourmet Coffee month, so rewards and recognitions given during January could have a coffee theme. Publicize the months and days you want to observe and then have employees come up with fun activities. Make a special note of any observances that are directly related to the work done within your organization. Make sure to have a celebration of all employees during those times.

Here is a partial list of some of the "months," "weeks," and "days" that exist.

January

1. Book Blitz Month (National)
2. Business & Reference Books Month
3. Careers in Cosmetology Month (National)
4. Clean Up Your Computer Month
5. Coffee Gourmet Month (International)
6. Hobby Month (US National)
7. Human Resource Month
8. Prune Breakfast Month
9. Tea Month (US National) – aka Hot Tea Month
10. Letter Writing Week - first week of January
11. Law Enforcement Training Week (National) - second week of January
12. Pizza Week (National) - second week of January
13. Book Week (National)
14. Handwriting Analysis Week (National) – observed the week containing January 23rd, John Hancock's Birthday.
15. Meat Week (National) - fourth week of January

February

16. African American History Month (Black History Month)
17. Bake For Family Fun Month
18. Bird Feeding Month (US National) (Wild Bird Feeding Month)
19. Candy Month
20. Chocolate Month
21. Friendship Month
22. Snack Food Month (US National)
23. Umbrella Month
24. School Counselors Week (National School Counseling Week) First week of February
25. Flirting Week - first week of February
26. Freelance Writers Appreciation Week – first week of February
27. Pancake Week - second week of February
28. National Pancake Day is Shrove Tuesday, the day before Lent.
29. Engineers Week (National) - third week of February
30. Random Acts of Kindness Week - third week of February

March

31. Craft Month
32. Frozen Food Month
33. International Hamburger & Pickle Month
34. Noodle Month
35. Peanut Month (National, US)
36. Social Worker's Month (National)
37. Federal Employees Recognition Week – first full week of March
38. Procrastination Week – second week of March
39. Egg Salad Week – full week after Easter Sunday

April

40. Frog Month (National)
41. Garden Month (National)
42. Guitar Month (International)
43. Humor Month (National)

44. Keep America Beautiful Month

45. Occupational Therapy Month

46. Welding Month (National)

47. Clean Out Your Refrigerator Week – first week of April

48. Astronomy Week – mid April sometime (depends on planetary alignment and such)

49. Wildlife Week (National) – third week of April

50. Administrative Professionals Week/Day (Formerly Professional Secretaries Week/Day) – last full week in April

May

51. Better Sleep Month

52. Egg Month (National)

53. Mental Health Awareness Month

54. Teacher Appreciation Month

55. Health Care Administrator's Week – first week of May

56. Teacher Appreciation Week (US National)

 – Tuesday of first full week of May

57. Gamblers Week – second week of May

58. Nurses Week (US National) – National Nurses Week is always observed May 6th thru May 12th (Florence Nightingale's birthday)

59. Police Week (National) – May 15 is National Peace Officers Memorial Day, and the week containing May 15 is National Police Week

60. Pickle Week (International) – fourth week of May

June

61. Candy Month

62. Dairy Month (National)

63. Flag Month (National)

64. Iced Tea Month (National)

65. People Skills Month (International)

66. Rose Month (National)

67. Turkey Lovers Month

68. Fishing Week (National) – first week of June

69. Bathroom Reading Week (National) – second week of June
70. Hug Week (National)
71. Camping Week (National) – fourth week in June

July

72. American Beer Month
73. Anti-Boredom Month
74. Baked Beans Month (National)
75. Blueberry Month (National)
76. Hot Dog Month (National)
77. Ice Cream Month (National)
78. Read An Almanac Month
79. Hug Week – third week of July
80. Salad Week (National) – fourth week of July

August

81. American Artist Appreciation Month
82. Inventors Month (US National)
83. Peach Month
84. Romance Awareness Month

85. Clown Week (US National) – August 1 - 7 each year
86. Smile Week (US National) – second week of August
87. Friendship Week (US National) – third week of August

September

88. Be Kind to Editors & Writers Month
89. Chicken Month (US National)
90. Classical Music Month
91. Coupon Month (US National)
92. Ethnic Foods
93. Hispanic Heritage Month
94. Jazz Month
95. Mushroom Month
96. Rice Month
97. Self-Improvement Month
98. Tiger Month
99. Women of Achievement Month
100. Assisted Living Week (US National) – second week in September

101. Rehabilitation Week (National) – third week in September

102. Singles Week (US National) – third week in September

103. Dog Week (US National) – last full week of September

104. Tolkien Week – last week in September

October

105. Book Month (National)

106. Bullying Prevention Month (National)

107. Caramel Month

108. Clock Month (US National)

109. Computer Learning Month

110. Cookie Month

111. Cosmetology Month (US National)

112. Country Music Month

113. Dental Hygiene Month (US National)

114. Drum Month (International)

115. Hispanic Heritage Month – mid-September to mid-October

116. Magazine Month (American)

117. Pasta Month

118. Physical Therapy Month (US National)

119. Pickled Pepper Month

120. Pregnancy & Infant Awareness

121. Sarcastic Awareness Month

122. Customer Service Week (National, US) – observed the first full week of October

123. Gerontological Nurses Week – first week of October

124. Get Organized Week – first week of October

125. Emergency Nurses Week – second week of October

126. Nephrology Technologist Week (National, US) – second week of October

127. Pet Peeve Week – second week of October

128. Teller Appreciation Week – second week of October

129. Business Women's Week (National Business Women's Week) – third week of October

130. Reading Week – third week of October

131. Character Counts Week (US National) – The Six Pillars of Character are: trustworthiness, respect, responsibility, fairness, caring and citizenship – fourth week of October

132. Magic Week – fourth week of October

133. Peace, Friendship & Goodwill Week – fourth week of October

November

134. Hospice Month (US National)

135. Native-American Heritage Month

(American Indian Heritage Month)

136. Medical Staff Services Week (US National) – first week of November

137. Allied Health Professions Week (US National) – second week of November

138. American Education Week – observed the full week prior to Thanksgiving.

139. Family Caregivers Week (US National) observed Thanksgiving Week

140. Family Week (US National) observed Thanksgiving Week

141. Game & Puzzle Week – fourth week of November

December

142. It's pretty much devoted to Christmas and Hanukkah

For more monthly, national celebrations, go to **www. nationaldaycalendar.com**. The website has a list of activities for every month and also every day of the year.

Chapter 8

Other Tips and Tricks for Improving Your Work Environment

Going beyond just choosing gifts or planning events is key to having a well-rounded, motivated workplace. This chapter will cover some general recognition ideas, staff communication solutions, suggestion box suggestions, and a few ways to increase public recognition.

General Recognition Ideas

These recognition ideas can be adapted in any way you see fit. The whole point of employee recognition is to recognize and reward those behaviors you desire. Once you have evaluated your company's needs and current recognition efforts, you should be able to take any or all of these ideas and create something that is uniquely effective for your specific workplace.

1. Give a percentage off of purchase of company-made products or services.

2. Give out points for good attendance or any other desirable activity. The points are redeemable for prizes.

3. Allow employees to participate in all personnel function decisions, hiring, training, evaluating, firing, and schedules.

4. Pick up your employees' mail and hand-deliver it.

5. Give out perfect attendance awards or certificates of achievement.

6. Provide a gift certificate to the employee with longest perfect attendance record.

7. Allow those with a perfect attendance record to enter a lottery for a $100 or $200 gift certificate.

8. Leave a message on an employee's voicemail thanking him for an outstanding job or contribution to the team.

9. Mention employees' success to your own boss. Make sure your superiors know what a great job your employees do of supporting your work efforts.

10. Fill a Bubble Gum machine with pink bubblegum and black bubblegum – employees earn tokens to try their luck at getting a black bubblegum, which earns them a reward.

11. Screen movies once a month in your boardroom or lunchroom. Pop popcorn and supply soda and licorice.

12. Reimburse employees for tuition fees for courses relevant to their work – this encourages professional development without restricting the course of study to areas you designate.

13. Set up a video game station – employees earn time to play the games.

14. Purchase a pinball or arcade game – employees earn tokens for free play.

15. Keep rolls of Lifesavers on hand. When you notice or hear about someone who really helped out in a particular situation, tie a thank you note to the roll.

16. Wash an employee's car out in the parking lot.

17. Change roles with an employee for the day.

18. Have only one designated parking spot in the parking lot – it is reserved for the employee of the month.

19. Hire temporary staff to cover essential duties when you hold meetings, conferences, or functions. This ensures all employees are able to attend, and no one feels left out.

20. Set up "Community Service" time where employees can use work hours to donate time to worthwhile charities or community activities.

21. Maintain a flower fund so you can send flowers to employees and their families when the need arises.

22. Let an employee attend a meeting in your place.

23. Give a dedicated worker a new title that better represents their contribution.

24. Host personal interest courses at lunchtime or directly after work. Examples include watercolor painting, fiction writing, cake decorating, and floral design.

25. Designate a VIP parking spot to an employee for a period of time.

26. Invite a deserving pet-lover to bring their pet to the office for the day.

27. Encourage a workaholic to leave a few hours early.

28. Set up a program and recruit employees to participate in a habitat for humanity project or other large charitable event. Encourage team and togetherness while benefiting a great cause.

29. Host an Employee Appreciation Day.

30. Sponsor an Employee Appreciation Week.

31. Put employees in TV commercials, training videos, or newspaper advertisements about your organization.

32. Host a surprise picnic for the entire team in the parking lot.

33. Create a "Hall Of Fame" wall with photos of outstanding achievements, both professional and personal.

34. Be your employees' champion at work. Stick up for them, and never make them scapegoats when a project did not meet expectations.

35. Reward employees with assignments you know they enjoy but don't get an opportunity to do regularly.

36. Reassign work that an employee does not enjoy.

37. Provide employees with more autonomy to determine how their work is to be completed.

38. Encourage employees to write their own personal mission statements. Have them share their statements at the next team or department meetings. Make sure you prepare one for yourself as well.

39. Hire additional staff for projects that require it.

40. Implement job sharing opportunities.

41. Provide flexible work schedules.

42. Rearrange your workspace so employees have more privacy.

43. Upgrade an employee's computer.

44. Upgrade an employee's office chair (executive, ergonomic, etc.).

45. Allow employees to rent art of their choice from a local art gallery for their office or work area.

46. Hold a steak-and-lobster feast after a particularly challenging project is completed.

47. Rotate jobs every hour on a designated day or days. This helps people understand what their colleagues actually do day to day.

48. Celebrate mistakes and near misses as well accomplishments and successes. Use the experience for everyone to learn and create a culture where it is OK to mess up every once in awhile. Give the person who made the mistake a special crown to wear, and discuss what could have been done to avoid the mistake; let everyone participate in the problem solving process.

49. Deliver an employee's paycheck in person and thank him for his dedication and commitment.

50. Write a note on an employee's paycheck envelope recognizing a particular accomplishment that week.

51. Rename one of the meeting rooms after the employee who has made the most notable contribution to the team during the previous 12 months.

52. Establish a "Q-Fund" – money can be used for anything that improves the overall quality of the employees life.

53. Host hikes, bike tours, walks, or sports games to promote teamwork and a family atmosphere.

54. Do laundry for employees – they drop it on Tuesday, pick it up on Wednesday folded, pressed, and crowned with a colorful lollipop on top.

55. Present a stuffed "Energizer bunny" to an employee who "keeps going and going."

56. Present a stuffed roadrunner to an employee who manages to complete a particular rush project in record time.

57. Have employees create a symbol of their team and put it on T-shirts, mugs, and caps.

58. At department meetings, have teams perform a skit related to their goals and objectives.

59. Lighten up on dress codes – insist on professional attire when meeting clients, but for days when employees will be in the office, let them wear jeans or a t-shirt.

60. Let an employee act as supervisor for a day – this is a reward, and it also increases awareness of and appreciation for the challenges you face on a daily basis.

61. Ask an employee to act as a mentor for a new employee.

62. Have employees develop presentations on what their job entails for other employees.

63. Name a day in someone's honor – you can play this up as much as you want to. Ideas include a recognition meeting with staff, a meal or cake, a gift presentation, a certificate presentation, or even a testimonial by an internal or external customer of the employee's exceptional value-laden work.

64. Sponsor an "Ideas Day" to recognize and generate new ideas – have employees spend an entire day examining ways to improve the way they worked.

65. Stock a "Thank You Store" and keep it full of quick and easy recognition items that managers, supervisors, and peers can use to reward other employees.

66. Keep pre-printed "you done good" or "a pat on the back" or "bravo" note cards on hand for managers, supervisors, and peers to inscribe whenever they see something recognition worthy.

67. Support a policy of promoting from within. This lets employees know that you value their history and dedication to the company.

68. Keep a four A's jar (Acknowledge, Appreciate, Affirm,

Assure). Fill it with wonderful, uplifting thoughts for anyone who needs one. You may also give these jars as gifts to your employees with one positive thought for every day of the year.

69. Have a circulating trophy or a "Pay it Forward" award. Each recipient is honored both in receiving the award, and then again in being able to select someone else they feel is worthy of some recognition.

70. Throw a company party in someone's honor to recognize a special achievement or service dedication.

71. Offer a training allowance that employees can use toward courses of their choice; for example, at the local junior college, university, or extension program.

72. Put a deserving employee in charge of something – a project, a special event, a team, etc.

73. Hold "Five-Minute Huddles" every day where team or department members regroup and outline exactly what needs to be done and by whom.

74. Share letters and feedback from appreciative clients. Read the notes aloud and post them in a prominent place.

75. Establish a "Caught in the Act" system where supervisors, managers, coworkers, etc. give out cards when they see great work being done. After accumulating 10 of these cards, the employee can "cash" them in for a reward.

76. Have employees come up with alternative job titles that are fun or better represent what they do in the company. For instance, a supervisor in accounting might want to call himself "Assistant to the Emperor of the Accounting Realm" or an administrative assistant might change her title to "Queen of Filedom." (Or, you might even go for something like "Assistant to the Regional Manager.") Have employees create business cards for their alter egos and use them with clients and visitors where appropriate.

Communication

Employees need to know what is going on within your organization. Keeping them in the loop is one of the best and least cumbersome ways to get the message out that you value them. Talk to employees on an informal basis every day, learn who they are, and share what you know about the company and its position. When you hold official meetings, employees should not be surprised by what they hear. If you are doing a good job keeping everyone informed, people will rally behind you in tough times and celebrate with you in good times.

1. Have regular teleconferences with all employees and support staff. Try to include the CEO and other senior management whenever possible.

2. Hold a regular meeting to tell staff what is going on and how they are doing.

3. Always hang charts, graphs, etc. to depict regularly how the company is doing.

4. Hold weekly meetings with small groups of employees to discuss anything that is on their minds.

5. Hold a weekly 20-minute meeting with one employee to discuss *anything* he or she wants.

6. Use face-to-face communication rather then email whenever you can.

7. Hold a regular meeting via Skype with any long-distance employees.

8. Make your memo, fax, and email templates interesting. Add cartoons or graphic designs to convey your personality as well as message.

9. Hold monthly employee meetings at which the financial performance of the previous month and other goals are discussed in detail.

10. Distribute daily reports of revenue performance – keep employees informed about the company's financial position.

11. Publish a regular employee newsletter and include some "fun" items as well as the must-read items.

12. When an employee submits a report for your review, write a personalized message on the report so the employee knows you actually read it.

13. When you bring visitors or clients to the office, make a point to introduce your employees, and have him explain what role he plays in bringing your product or service to market.

14. When people in your organization first turn on their computers, have a message of the day pop up. You can use a quotation on customer service, personal growth, something humorous, or even the birthdays of employees during that week.

15. Skip the formalities in your letters and memos. Stop using words and phrases like heretofore, therein, hereby, please be advised, sincerely, etc. Use words that you would hear in conversation. It improves your image and makes you more accessible.

16. Circulate customer letters praising fellow coworkers, scan them, and email the file to everyone or print them in the company newsletter. Make sure everyone sees the positive feedback, and encourage everyone to congratulate the employee mentioned.

17. When someone within the company or a client says something positive about one of your employees, convey the message back to that employee as soon as possible. Thank him for making you look good.

18. Place congratulatory letters in employee's files.

19. Use your newsletter to introduce individual employees to the rest of the organization. Interview the employee and find out what interests them, if they have any special hobbies or talents, and what generally makes them tick.

20. Host monthly breakfasts for employees to gather together and learn what is new and coming down the pipe.

21. Use different exits and entrances for work every day. This way, you will meet new people on a regular basis.

22. Make a point to visit the office or workspace of someone you don't have much direct interaction with.

23. Schedule short meetings with another manager's employees. Use the time to learn about opportunities and challenges in other departments.

24. Give employees access to files pertaining to their work history, their jobs, and their department. Create an environment of openness where information is accessible to all and not held by only a few "chosen" ones.

25. Move your office or workspace out of the corner and relocate to smack-dab in the middle of everything. You'll be surprised at the increased interaction and information you glean, which will help you do your job better and at the same time communicate to your employees that you are one of them.

26. Communicate regularly on messaging, video, or imaging apps. These can be fun and creative.

27. Talk, talk, talk, talk, talk, and talk some more!

Suggestion Box

Suggestions from employees should not be viewed as necessary evils. Often, the best ideas come from those who work with the process and procedures every day. Find ways to encourage suggestions, and make sure your system has a mechanism to acknowledge all suggestions received.

1. Always find ways to get staff's input into the operation – just a simple suggestion box works great. Make sure pens and paper are handy!

2. Work hard at finding a way to implement each suggestion, and give a clear explanation as to why it cannot be used if that is the case.

3.   Acknowledge all suggestions, even if not implemented, and express appreciation for the thought that went into preparing the idea.

4.   If you do implement an employee's suggestion, make sure you publicize it, and consider giving a reward.

5.   For suggestions that are implemented and that result in cost cuts, award a percentage of the money saved to the employee who made the suggestion.

6.   Sponsor "The Great Idea Award" complete with certificate, pin, and an award or gift. If possible, name the improvement or idea after the employee, and let customers who are affected by the improvement know who was behind the suggestion.

7.   Hold an annual draw of all suggestions received. The winner receives a reward.

8.   Always ask for input on cost-cutting measures.

9.   Create an "Awesome Attempt" booklet of great ideas that just weren't implementable or feasible at the time. This way, the employee's efforts are appreciated, and your organization has a record of ideas it can turn to in the future.

Publicity

People vary in the amount of publicity they want for their accomplishments. You need to respect each employee's comfort level with public praise. For those that thrive on publicity, you can really pour it on, and for those who shy away from the limelight, share their accomplishments with others in a low-key manner. Recognition will quickly lose its value if it is done without regard for an employee's feelings, so always keep that in mind before you single someone out for worthy accolades.

1.   At the end of the workday, plan an employee recognition ceremony. Hold it in your conference room, kitchen, or

largest office space. Give an announcement/speech about the completed project and give recognition to the people who made it possible.

2. Stand in front an employee's desk and in a loud voice, read a "decree" from a scroll of their accomplishment. Give all your "winners" paper crowns to wear for the day along with a reward.

3. Get on the company intercom and announce the people and teams who reached their goal. Have the winners meet you in the conference room, lunchroom, etc. for a short reception to celebrate the accomplishment!

4. Buy a local billboard to celebrate a person's professional accomplishments and distinguished service to your organization and its clients.

5. Implement a Wall of Fame, Tower of Power, Pillars of Pride or equivalent methods to showcase and publicize your employee's achievements, recognition events, and celebrations. These displays can be in the building lobby or in your reception area – anywhere where they will be seen by clients and visitors to your organization. Remember to update the display regularly, and keep it current and relevant. Outdated and obsolete information will detract from, rather than support, your recognition efforts.

6. Take out a full-page ad in newspaper or local magazine once a year thanking employees, and name each of them individually.

7. Start a column in your newsletter for employee recognition. Send the newsletter to clients, and keep a few extra copies to give to the employee mentioned.

8. Tell the employees' clients about the recognition they received. Explain what the recognition was for and thank the client for their continued support.

9. Create a "Tree of Appreciation" for all staff to post congratulations, kudos, and thank yous to employees who make a difference. Place the tree in a prominent spot.

10. Write a "Friday Fan Mail" where you thank an employee for his weekly contributions and accomplishments. Send the email to everyone in the organization.

11. Post a thank-you note on the recipient's office door.

12. Send an email message to everyone in the company advising of someone's personal contribution to your own accomplishment.

13. Create a "Behind the Scenes" Award for those who tend to shun the limelight.

14. Post on your company's social media accounts. Whatever platform you're on, feature an employee who deserves to be seen all over the internet. It could be a picture, quick video, or short post about the person's accomplishments.

Chapter 9

Final Staffing Thoughts

In order to keep the motivation at a high level, you have to ensure that your staff is on board – from new hires to senior management. This chapter will take a look at several tactics and approaches, from ensuring that your new hires understand the motivational environment of your workplace to making sure that senior management is continuously involved.

Orientation/New Employees

At no time is personal and meaningful recognition more important than when a new employee enters your workplace. First impressions really are everything, and if you relay the message loud and clear from day one that your employees are important, those employees will feel important and engaged right from the start. Orientation is so often neglected, and managers need to realize the significance that effective orientation has on future work performance and motivation.

1. Have several line staff call the new hire to welcome him to the team the day before he or she starts.

2. Have the General Manager spend at least an hour with every new employee.

3. Give every employee printed business cards.

4. Develop a welcoming ceremony.

5. Send new employee flowers on first day.

6. Send new employees on a scavenger hunt – they have to find certain places and items within the office or building.

7. Create special new employee shirts – other employees who see someone wearing this shirt must introduce themselves.

8. Create a collection of company legends and success stories on video or audiotape. Use these tapes as a source of pride for current employees and as a wonderful addition to orientation for new hires.

9. Create a public post of videos and/or pictures on your company's social media pages, website, or blog.

10. Create a "Soft Landings" welcome kit that is already on their desk when they begin their first day. Include necessary office supplies, a phone list, employee list, and a special treat.

Senior Management Involvement

Senior management support and buy-in to recognition efforts is critical for recognition to be perceived as anything more than a perfunctory gesture from the managers and supervisors. The impact of a senior official's recognition for a job well done will almost always outweigh the impact of the same message delivered by the employee's day-to-day manager. It's not fair, but it's the truth. The perception is, "If these high up people take the time to thank me, I must be doing something right!" Don't fight this natural tendency: exploit it, and use senior management participation to make a significant impact on your recognition and motivation efforts.

11. Have senior managers cook employees breakfast.

12. Have senior managers bring around an ice cream cart.

13. Have senior managers serve employees donuts and coffee.

14. Have senior managers wash the windshields of employees' cars as they arrive at work.

15. Have senior managers take all employees to lunch.

16. Have senior managers make spontaneous calls to line staff saying how much they are appreciated, and give specific reasons why.

17. Host a "Meet the President" forum for lunch. Make sure most employees can attend.

18. Reward employees with a lunch with the top departmental administrator.

19. Extend invitations to deserving employees to participate in "higher-level" meetings.

20. Hold an annual banquet for those with more than a certain number of years of service.

21. Implement management reviews where the employees assess their manager's and supervisor's performance.

22. Hand out VIP passes that allow an employee access to otherwise reserved areas within your company.

23. Set aside a day where senior managers perform front line jobs. This is a great opportunity to interact with employees, and it keeps upper management in touch with the day-to-day opportunities and challenges faced by line staff.

24. Hold regular face-to-face information sessions with employees, and answer any and all questions that come up.

Chapter 10

FAQs About Reward and Recognition

1. What can I do to reward my employees?

While monetary reward is typically the first answer that comes to mind, they are not the only (or even the most) effective recognition strategy for motivating your staff. Using monetary rewards is not always possible, and employees can come to expect gifts rather than "thanks," which puts you in a tough situation.

2. If I have no money to reward my employees, what can I do?

There are so many non-monetary and low cost ways to recognize and reward employees. I have included 508 specific ideas for recognition, but the most important factors for employee recognition are at the beginning of the book where you will learn to create a motivating foundation. Once you have done that, rewards are just the icing on the top — nice to look at, sweet to taste, but the cake underneath is the really good part.

3. When I try to complement or recognize my employees for little things, some of them act uncomfortable. Am I doing it right?

In order for recognition to be effective, you need to consider the following three elements of the person and your relationship with him or her:

- **Does that individual employee value the way you are recognizing him or her?**

    All people respond differently to positive feedback, some get a real boost of pride and others shy away and are embarrassed. You need to know your employees' personalities and tailor your recognition efforts accordingly.

- **Does the recognition you are providing have to do with an activity or accomplishment the employee actually values?**

    When people think you are just saying something nice because you have to, the compliment is often interpreted as an insult. "If you can't find something good to say about my work that really matters to me, that must mean I'm not doing a good job." Make sure your recognition efforts are genuine and specific to your employee's work.

- **Do you have a positive relationship with the employee you are trying to recognize?**

    Hearing a compliment from someone you trust and respect is much better received than one from someone you find difficult to get along with. Try to establish personal, meaningful relationships with all of your employees while still respecting their personal boundaries and comfort zones.

When you address the three elements above, you should see a marked difference in the way your recognition is received.

4. When I publicly highlight someone's work, other employees say they feel unappreciated.

The most likely cause for this is that those other employees are feeling underappreciated and not recognized. Make an effort to find something positive to say about everyone everyday. You aren't obligated to keep checklists of who got recognized for what and when, but it is important to find something positive to say about everyone on a regular basis.

5. I like to recognize my employees, but my own supervisor doesn't do much recognizing of his own. What can I do to get some praise myself?

A great method to try is to recount some of your recognition efforts to your boss. Talk to him about the effectives of your recognition and how it has made your job much easier. Serve as a role model of recognition for your boss by recognizing his efforts. Recognition is infectious. You will see that he or she is much more likely to return the thanks when he realizes how good it made him feel inside to receive your compliments.

6. What should I do when it's obvious that only some staff are doing the work of the team and I want to recognize the team effort?

This is a tough situation and one where you need to first address why some employees are doing all the work. Perhaps you need to take a more hands-on approach and coach the slackers to improve their performance. When you know there is disparity of effort within a team, honor the team in a small way and then provide individual recognition and reward at will. You can celebrate the team's results and reward individual contributions at the same time.

7. My staff wouldn't take me seriously if I all of sudden started praising them and thanking them. What do I do?

If you haven't been a "recognizer" in the past, then this transformation should be managed just as any other change initiative within your organization. Start by communicating why recognition is important and then discuss how you intend to start implementing the program. Start off low key and gradually build yourself up to singing their praises from the rooftops. When your employees get a first-hand glimpse at how it feels to be recognized for both large and small accomplishments, they will wonder why they thought it was foreign in the first place.

8. What should I recognize? Excellence? Customer Service? Performance Improvement? Cost-saving?

The only rule to follow is this: "What gets recognized gets done." If you want more cost savings, then start recognizing the heck out of anything your employees do to achieve it. If you want customer service excellence, then catch employees doing something nice for customers. Make sure your recognition has a direct link to the behavior you are encouraging. Don't just say, "thanks," say, "Thank you for helping that customer find exactly what she was looking for. I'm sure you improved her shopping experience tenfold."

9. I am not comfortable organizing or hosting parties or public events. How can I recognize my employees?

There are lots of other ways to recognize your employees that don't involve parties or public events. You employees will probably know and realize that you are not a high publicity type and would not expect such recognition from you in the first place. If you think your staff would enjoy a party, solicit them to plan the event. A party is fun no matter who organizes it, and the activity will give them a refreshing break form their daily routines.

10. How do I know if I'm recognizing people the right way?

You will know your recognition is working by three main criteria:

- Is the person receiving the recognition displaying positive and open body language?

- Has the work place improved in terms of comfort and increased performance?
- Do you feel good after giving the recognition?

If you answer "yes" to the above questions, then your recognition efforts are working. If there is something lacking, go directly to the source and ask your employees what you could do better. Perhaps you are not as in-tune with their individual needs, preferences, and values as you need to be in order to deliver effective praise. Your recognition efforts will need to change and adapt on a regular basis, so get used to soliciting feedback on your recognition technique, and put the suggestions into action.

Conclusion

Well — there you have it: tons of ways to help you get your creative juices flowing when it comes to unique, fun, practical, and sincere ways to recognize your employees and create a high motivation workplace.

We started off this discussion about motivation by discussing intrinsic motivation and have come full circle to end with extrinsic motivators. The whole point of this book is that you can't isolate these different frames of reference. They work very interdependently with intrinsic motivation forming the foundation for extrinsic motivation to be built upon. It's not enough to simply throw rewards at employees and expect them to respond positively. Your entire culture must be built on recognition and appreciation. Some forms of recognition are extrinsic, but the more lasting elements are those that permeate to the core of your business philosophy and values.

Armed with the information, tools, and techniques of this newly revised book, I hope you are no longer on a search for "motivated employees" and that you understand the necessity of first building a motivating environment. I'm reminded of the line from the movie *Field of Dreams*, "Build it and they will come." It's true — if you set your workplace up as a motivational place, the people within will become motivated in the direction you desire, and the people you bring in will be attracted to your workplace because of the culture and atmosphere you create.

Remember: You don't *find* motivated employees; you *provide motivating environments* for employees.

I sincerely hope you now have a response to the question I posed to you at the very beginning of this book:

"How motivated are you to provide a motivating workplace?"

Glossary

Effective recognition – can be defined as "motivation that increases the self-esteem and initiative of the recipient, resulting in a lasting improvement in their behavior and performance which positively impacts the bottom line."

ERG Theory of Needs – motivational theory developed by Clayton Alderfer with three groups of needs that individuals move through to become motivated: 1) existence, 2) relatedness, and 3) growth.

External motivators – consists of those things that the world offers in response to an individual's inner drives; these can be considered the enticements an employer offers to its employees such as salary, benefits, recognition, and advancement.

Extrinsic outcomes – work related conditions, salary, and security are the expected outcomes or rewards.

Four Drive Model Theory – holistic way of looking at employee motivation beyond the typical "pay" model that most corporate businesses use today.

Gain sharing – This compensation method divides the results of improved performance between the employer and employees.

Hygiene and motivational factors – those elements of a job that are related to working conditions and motivational factors that relate to elements that enrich one's job.

Internal motivators – influences that propel an individual to pursue a certain job, type of career, education or other activity; these inner drives provide people with their most basic form of satisfaction.

Intrinsic motivators – how interesting, challenging, and meaningful the job is.

Job enrichment – a type of job redesign that is intended to address the effects of boredom, lack of flexibility, and employee dissatisfaction that result from work tasks that are repetitive and highly directed.

Job rotation – the movement between different jobs in order to increase interest and motivation.

Management by objective (MBO) – a management method developed by Peter Drucker that advocates a participative goal-setting process that actively involves managers and subordinates at every level in the organization.

Management methods – the managerial policies and practices accepted and endorsed by the organization, its values, and culture.

Motivation – the reason or reasons one has for acting or behaving in a particular way.

Motivation theories – theories developed and studied by professionals that analyze individual and group motivation.

Participative management – the idea of utilizing the knowledge, strengths, creativity, and ingenuity of all employees within an organization and not simply relying on the managers and supervisors to direct work.

Performance-based pay – based on paying the worker for his or her unique value, rather than assessing a value to the job itself.

Performance bonus – this type of bonus can be based on individual or group performance.

Profit sharing – these compensation systems are not related to an individual's performance, but are linked to the profits of an enterprise.

Recognition – external motivator that applies to everyone; acknowledgement of something or someone's existence, validity, or legality.

Self-directed work teams – a group of people who combine different skills and talents to work toward a common purpose or goal.

Six factors of effective recognition – following six basic factors of effective recognition: genuine, spontaneous, personal, specific, timely, and public.

Skill-based pay – refers to a pay system in which pay increases are linked to the number or depth of skills an employee applies to his or her job.

Spiral Dynamics – explores the core values and thoughts that drive individual's beliefs and actions.

The job characteristics model – a program that allows management to analyze and design jobs.

"The management" – the beliefs, values, personality, capabilities, etc. that influence the actions of each manager, leader, and supervisor within the organization.

"The managed" – the beliefs, values, personality, capabilities, etc. that influence the way each employee within the organization desires to be managed and his reactions to the current management style.

"The work" – the actual work that needs to be done within the organization to ensure sustainability and/or profitability.

vMEMEs – value systems are combined with memes (cognitive or behavioral pattern that can be transmitted from one individual to another one) to form nine different vMEMEs, and by discovering which vMEME an individual operates under, others can relate better to that individual.

Vroom's Expectancy Theory of Motivation – a motivational theory based on the idea that individuals have expectations about outcomes and that, in terms of work, there are two main groups of outcomes: intrinsic outcomes and extrinsic outcomes.

Bibliography

Emelander, Stan. Management Articles. *The Four Drive Theory in the Workplace*. 2009. **www.managerwise.com**

Nelson, Kurt. Lantern Group. *4-Drive Model: New Theory on Employee Motivation*. **http://lanterngroup.com**

Society of Human Resource Management. Executive Summary: Employee Job Satisfaction Survey. 2015. **www.shrm.org**

TINYpulse. The 7 Key Trends Impacting Today's Workplace: Results from the 2014 TINYpulse Employee Engagement and Organizational Culture Report. 2014. **www.tinypulse.com**

Index